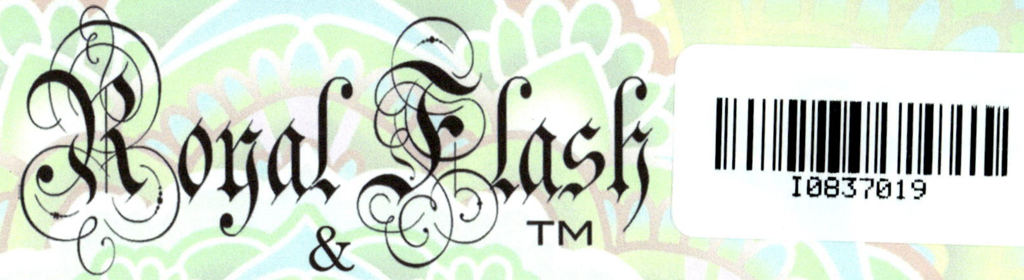

&

Cort's Royal Ink Tattoo Company

Presents

"101 Colorful Mandala's"

ISBN: 978-1-948187-28-2

All artwork by

Cort Bengtson

Published by Cort's Royal Ink Tattoo Company

Book Design and Layout by Cort Bengtson

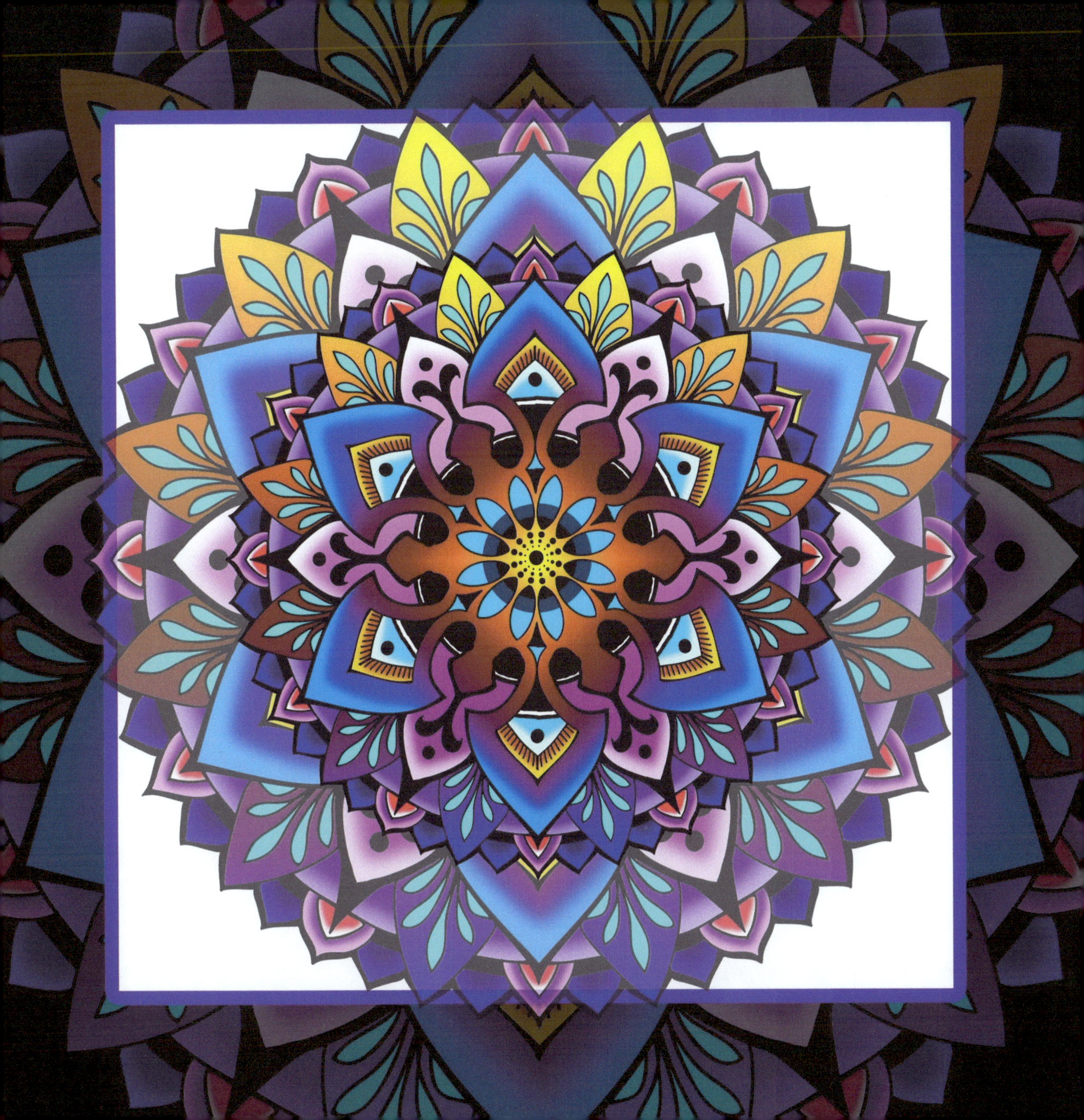

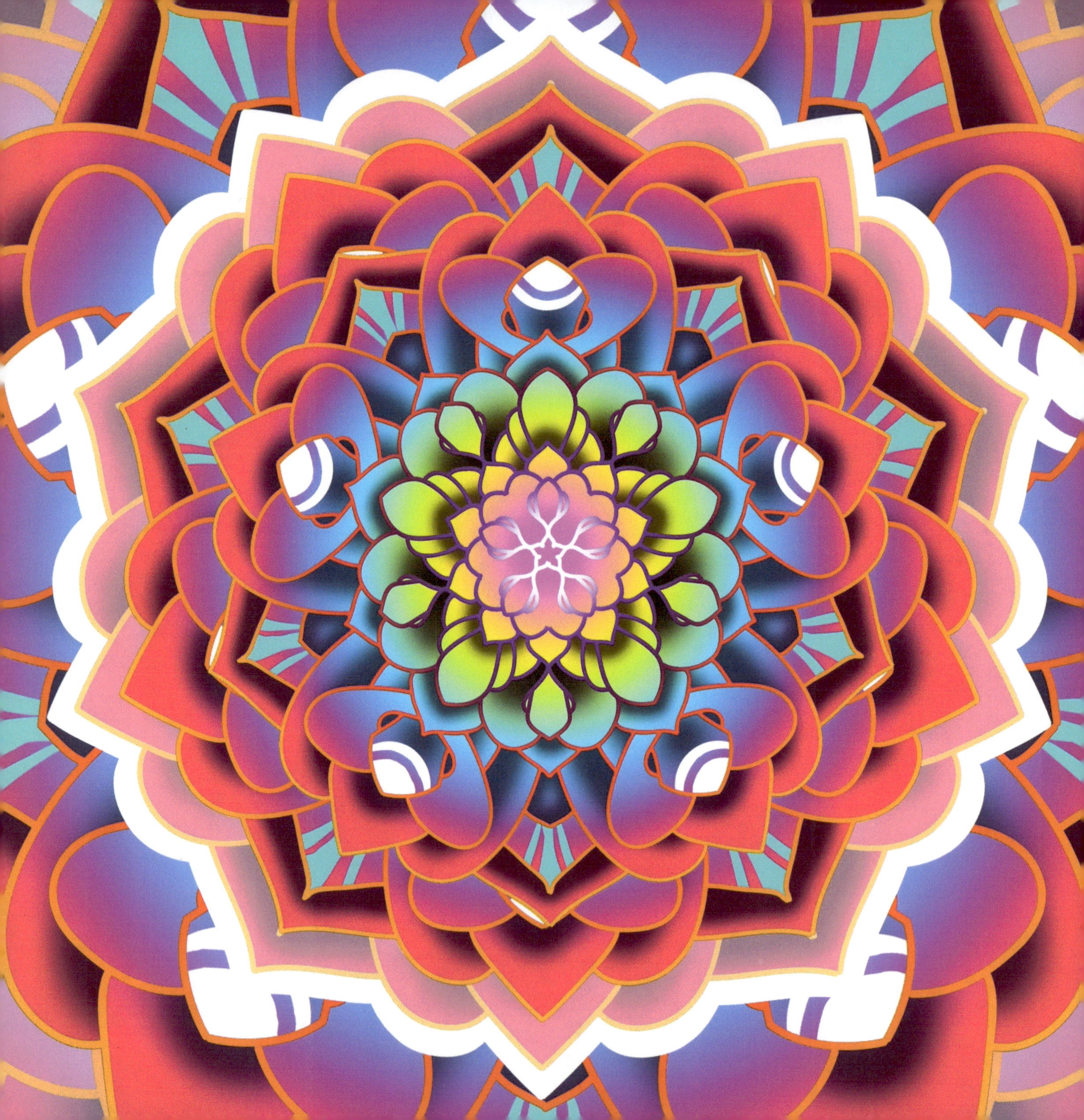

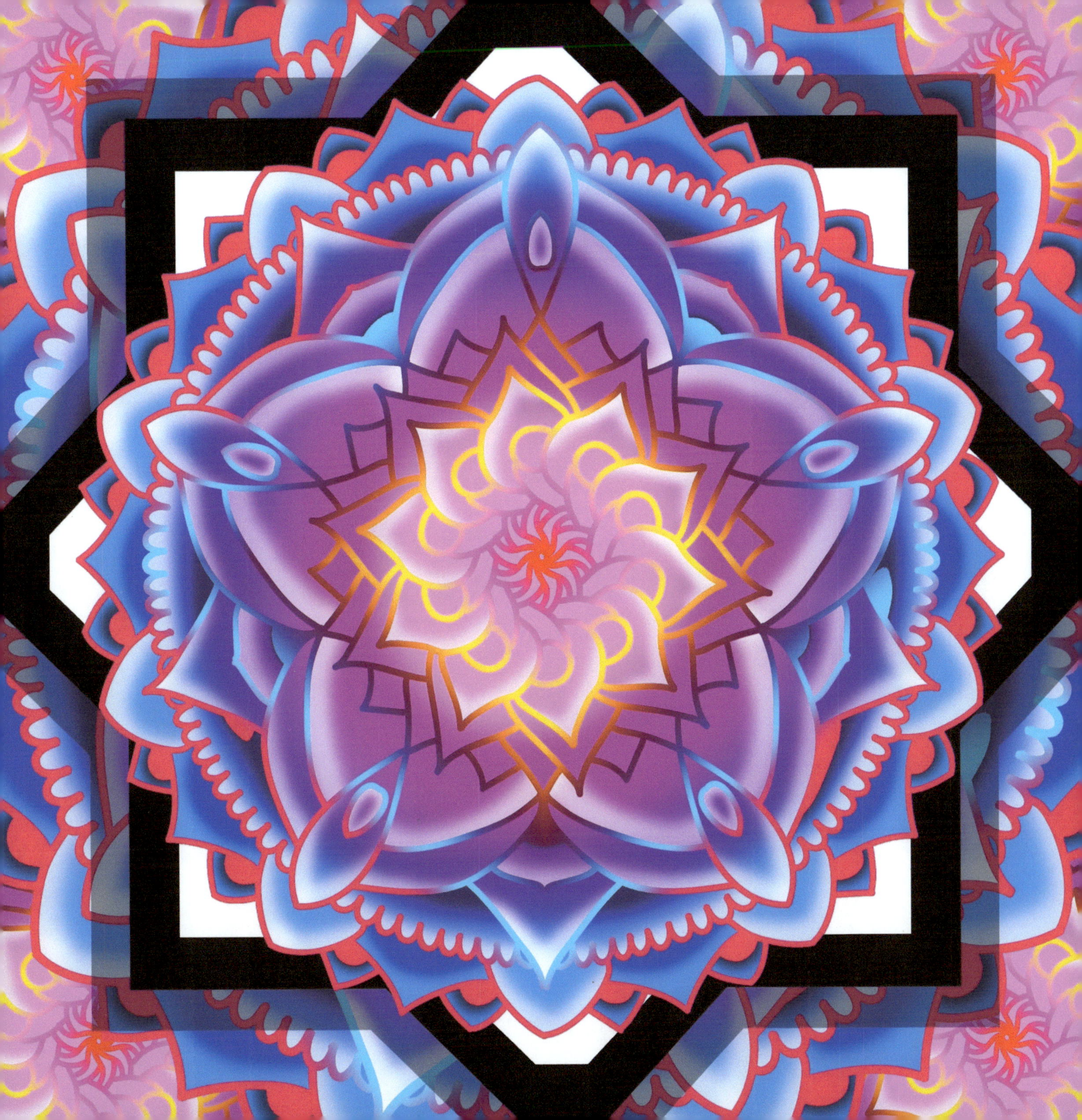

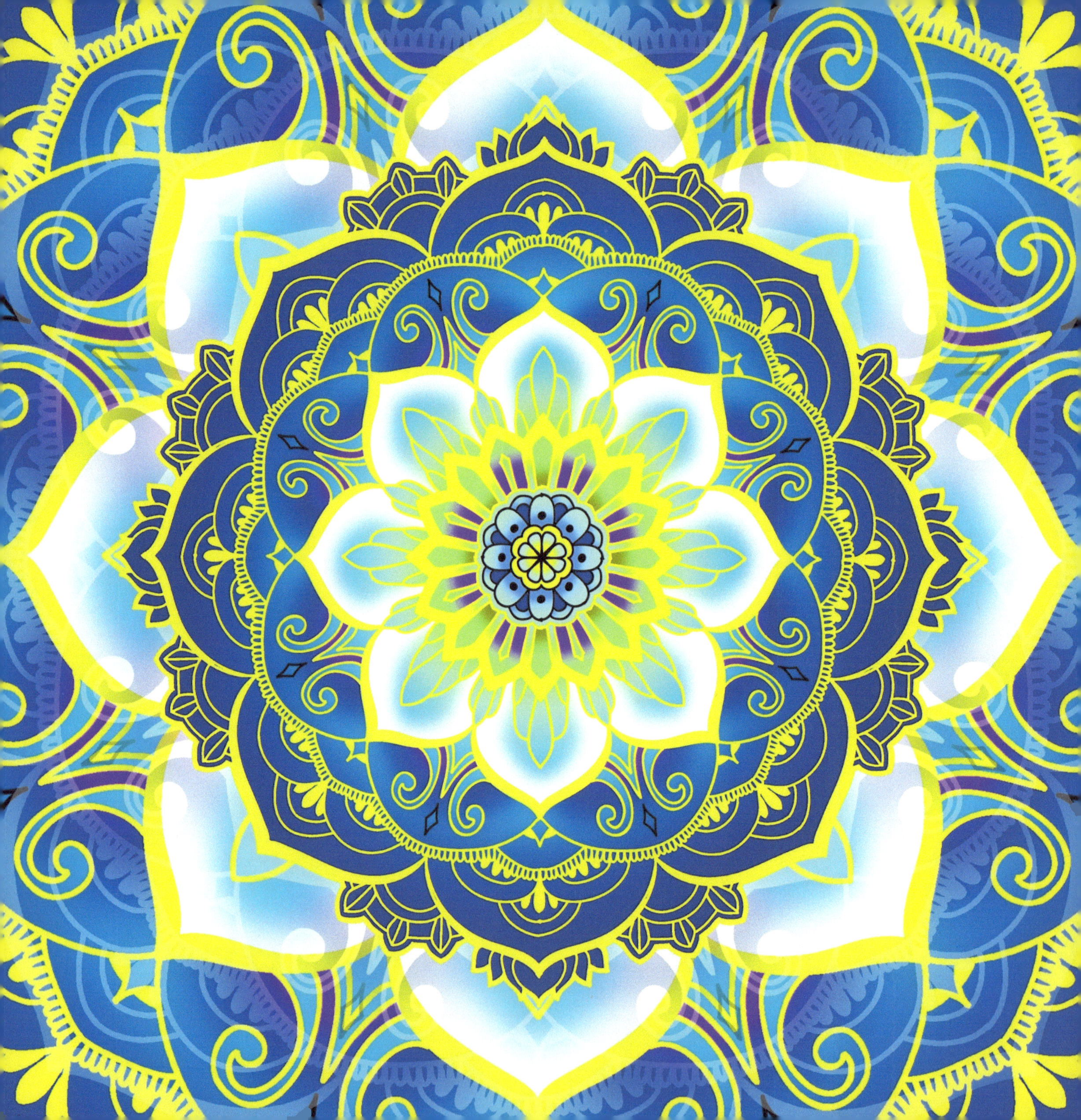

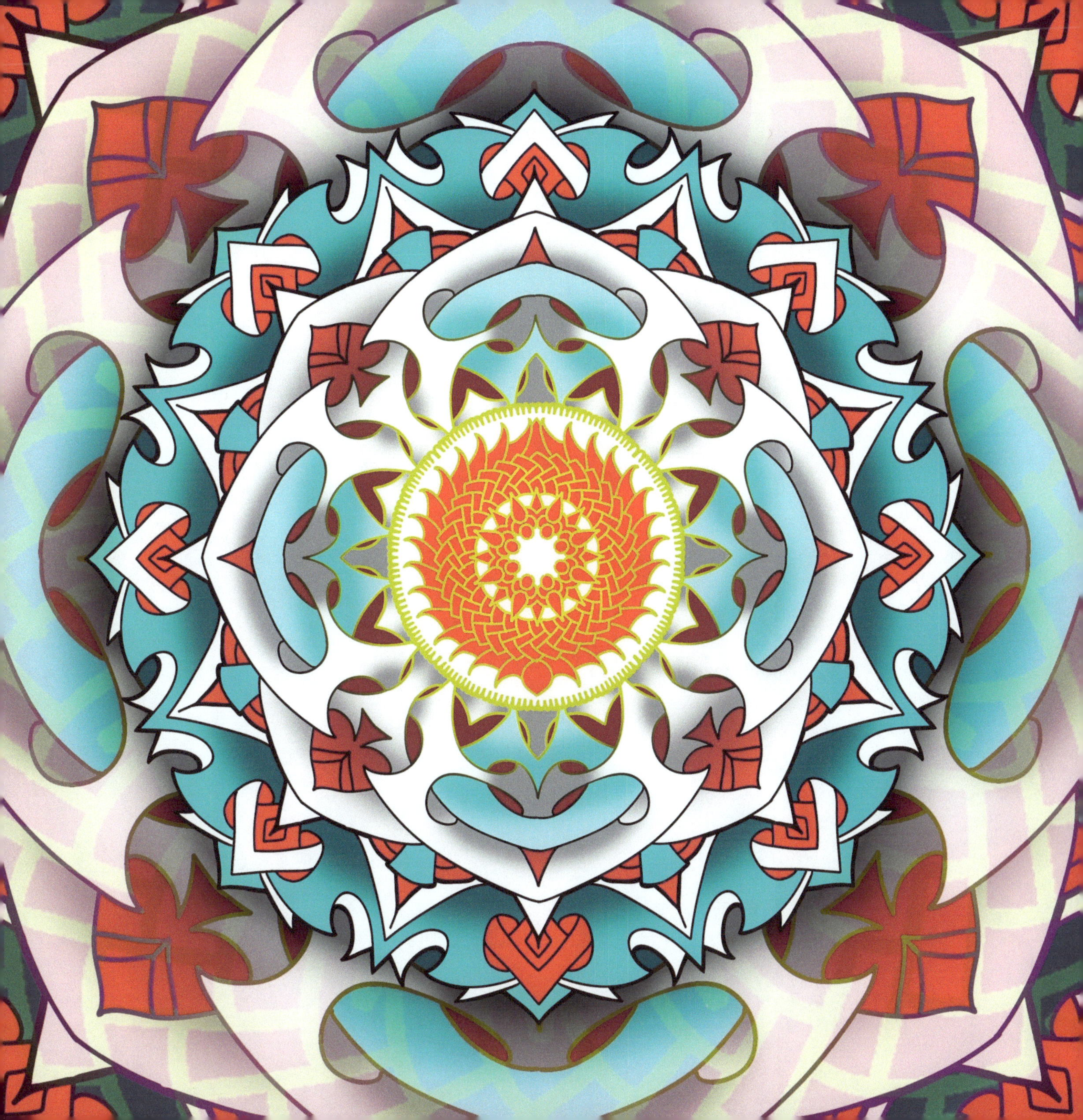

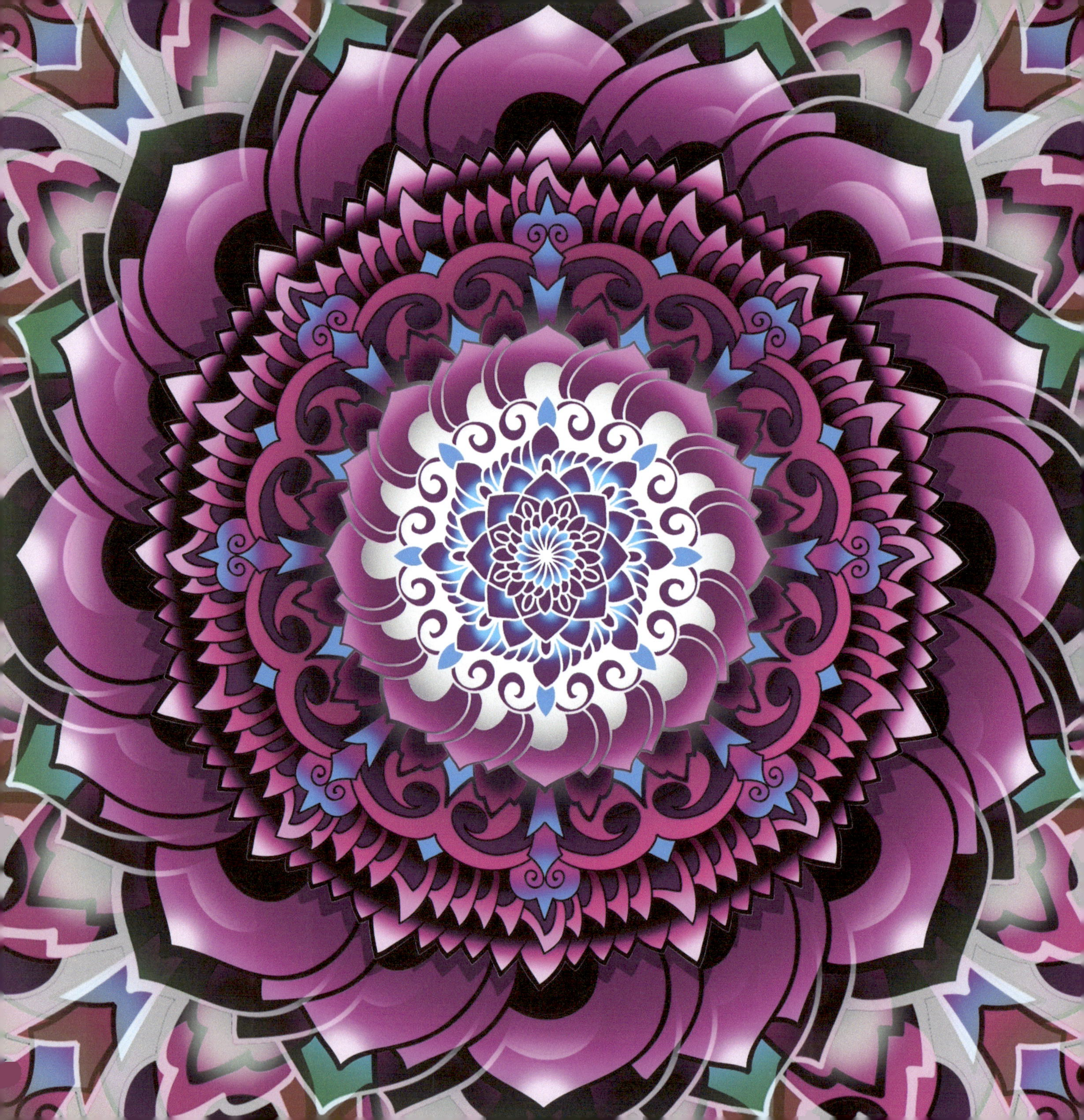

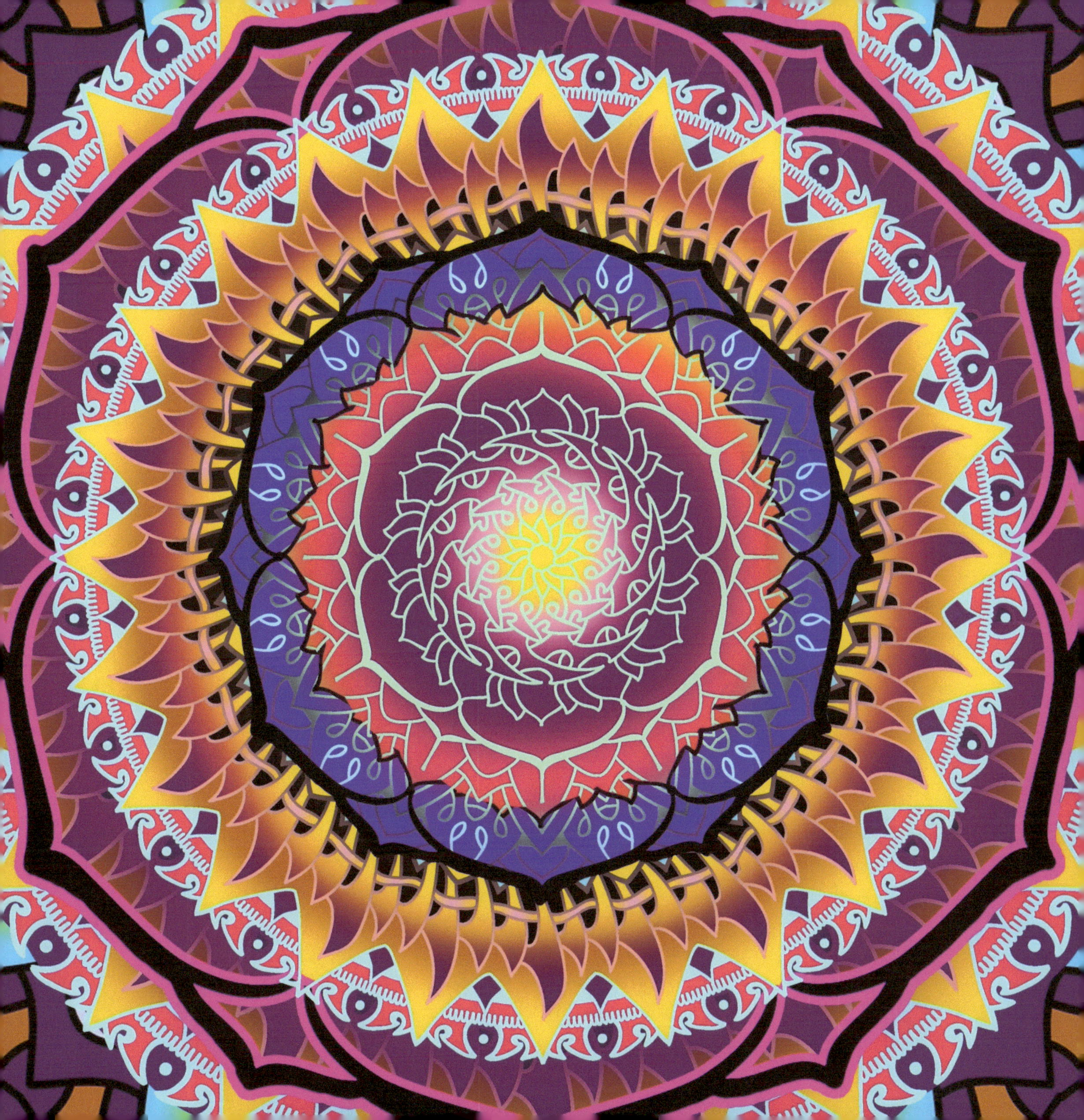

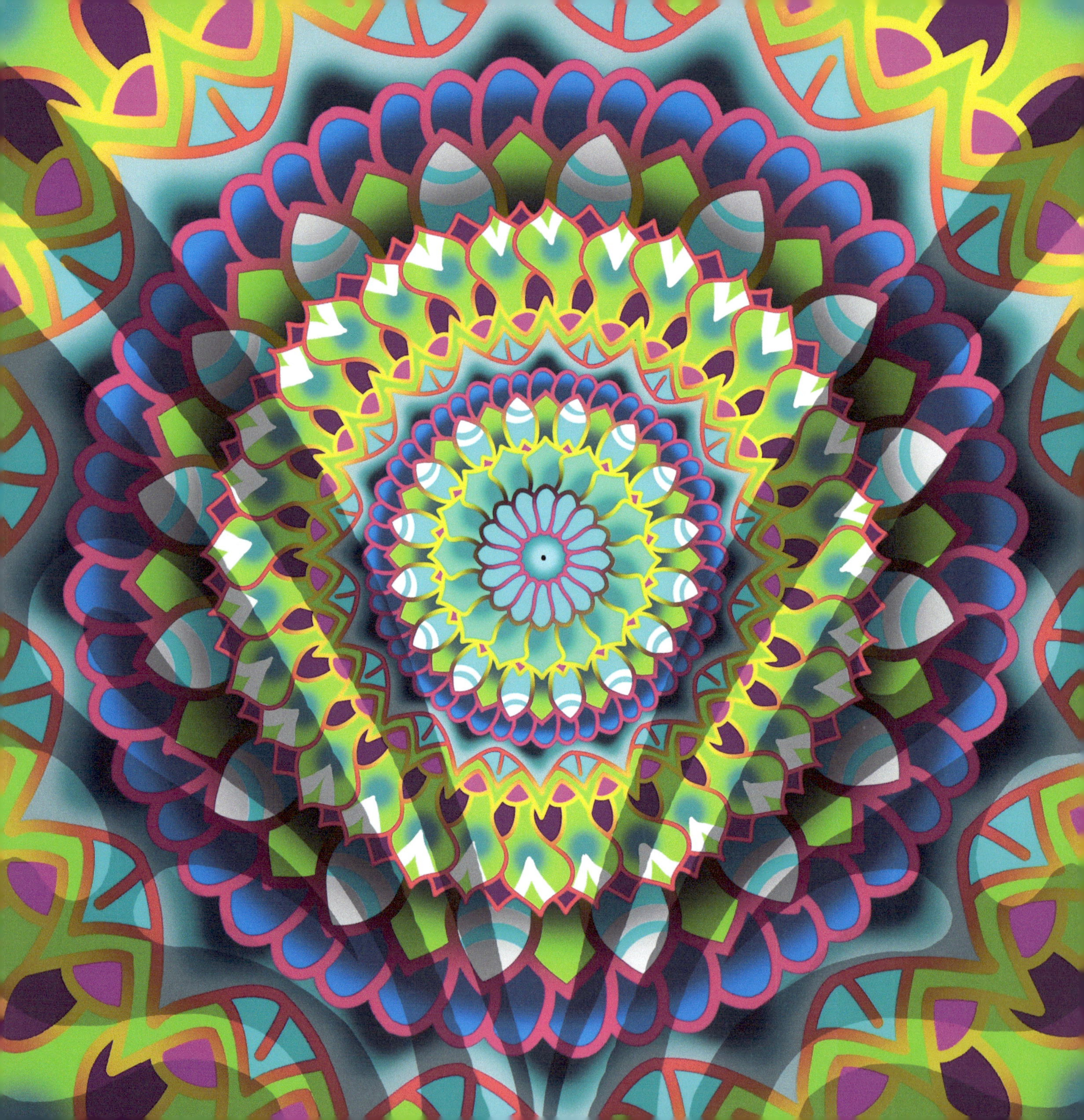

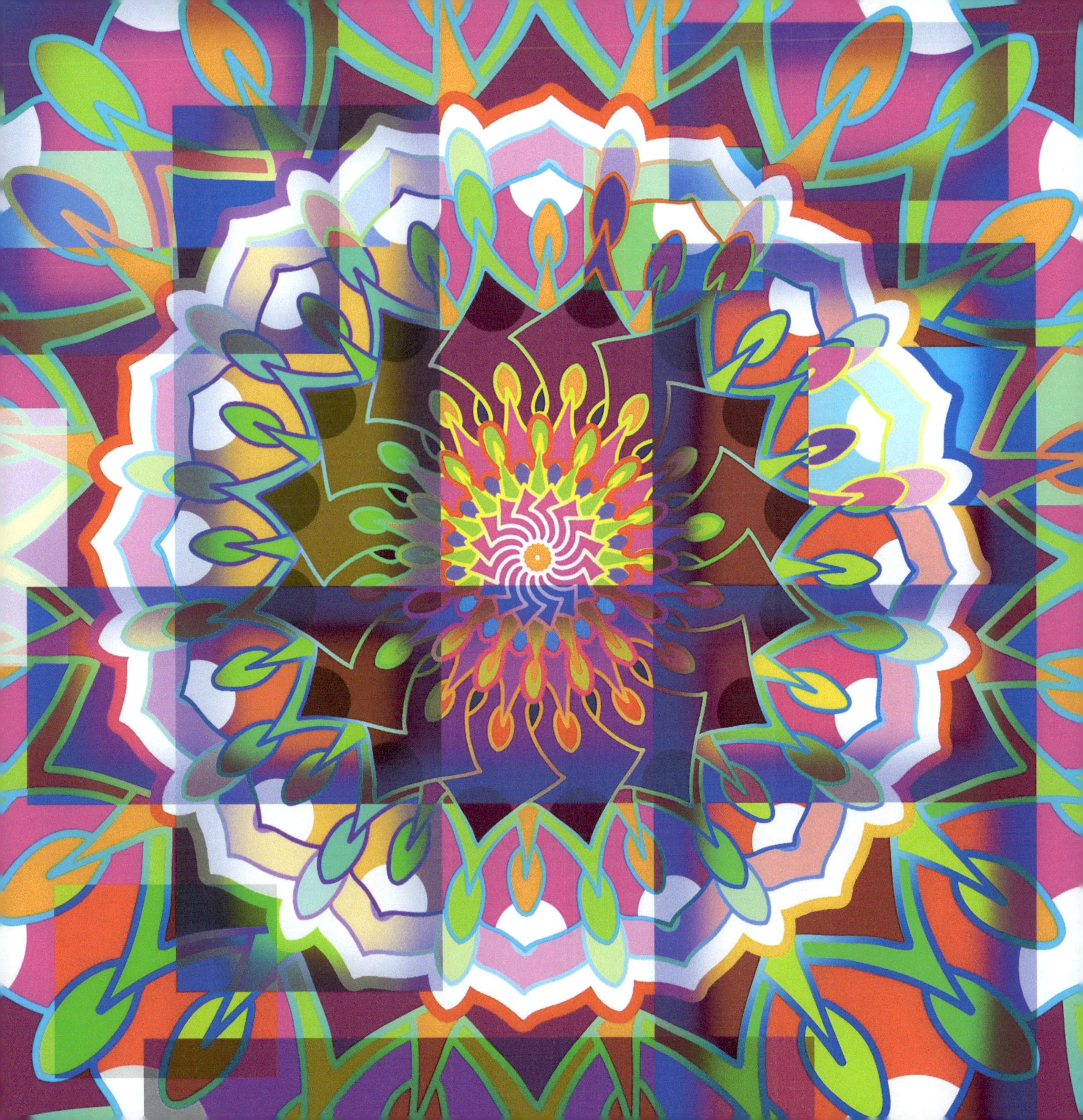

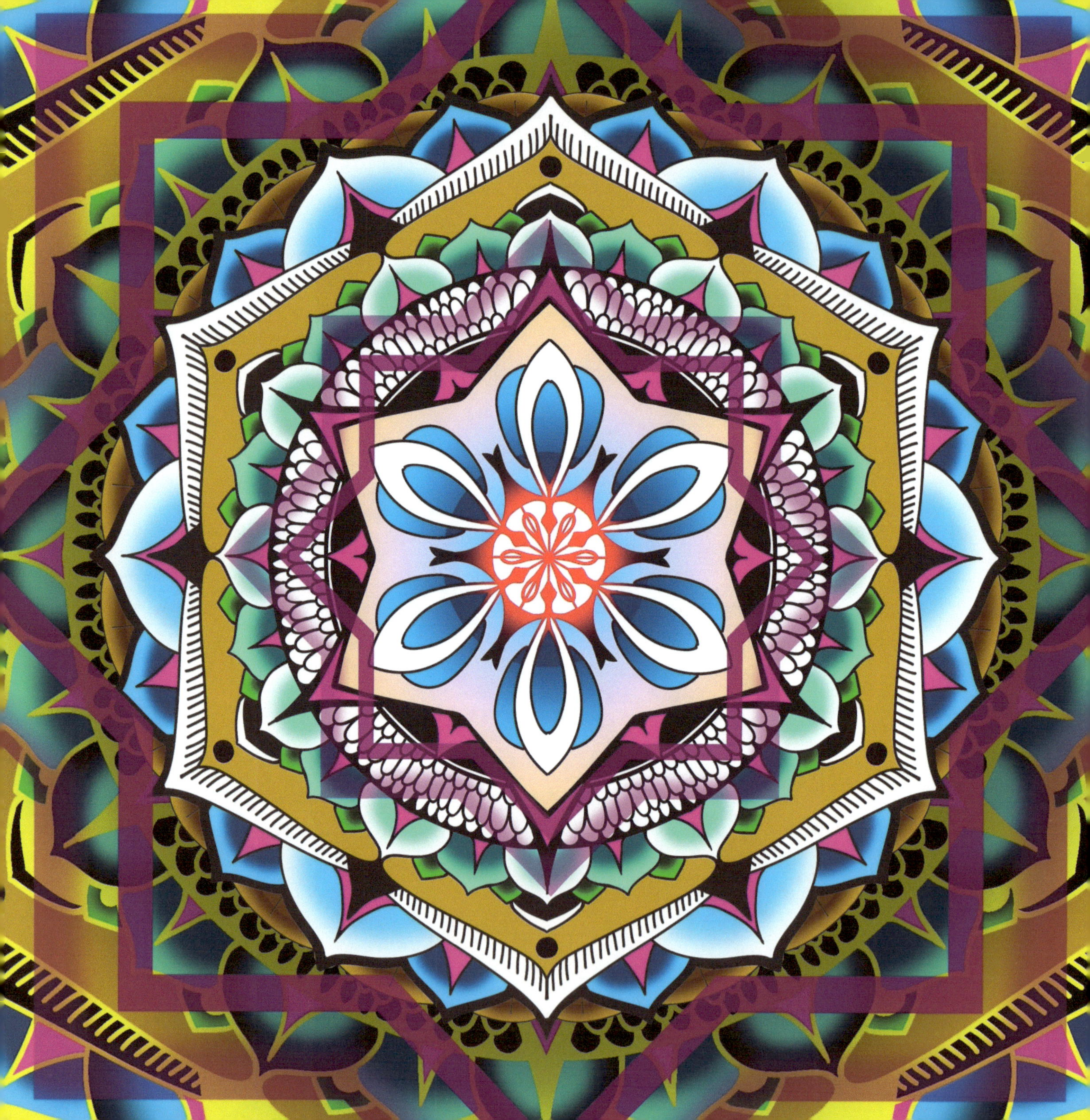

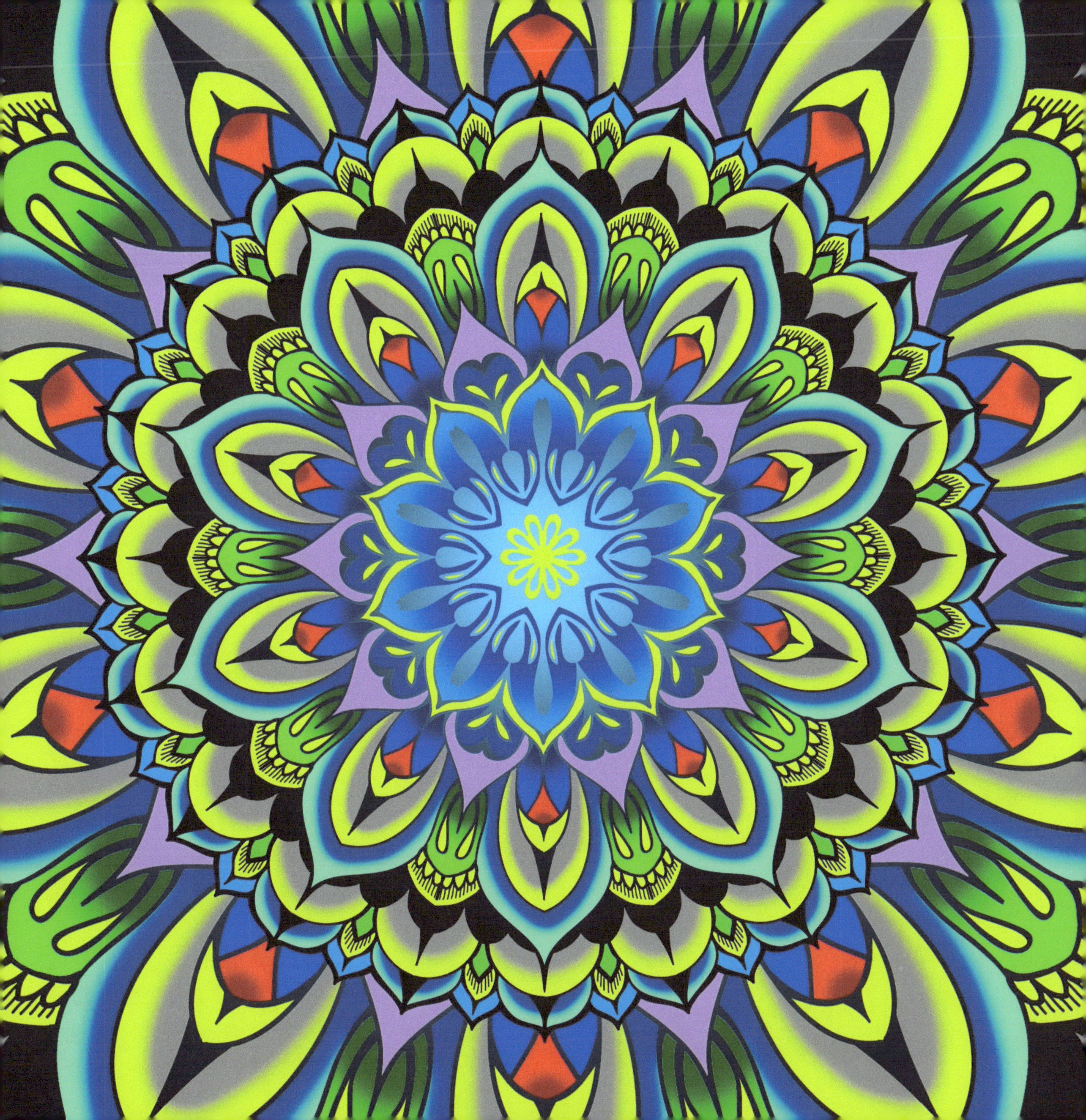

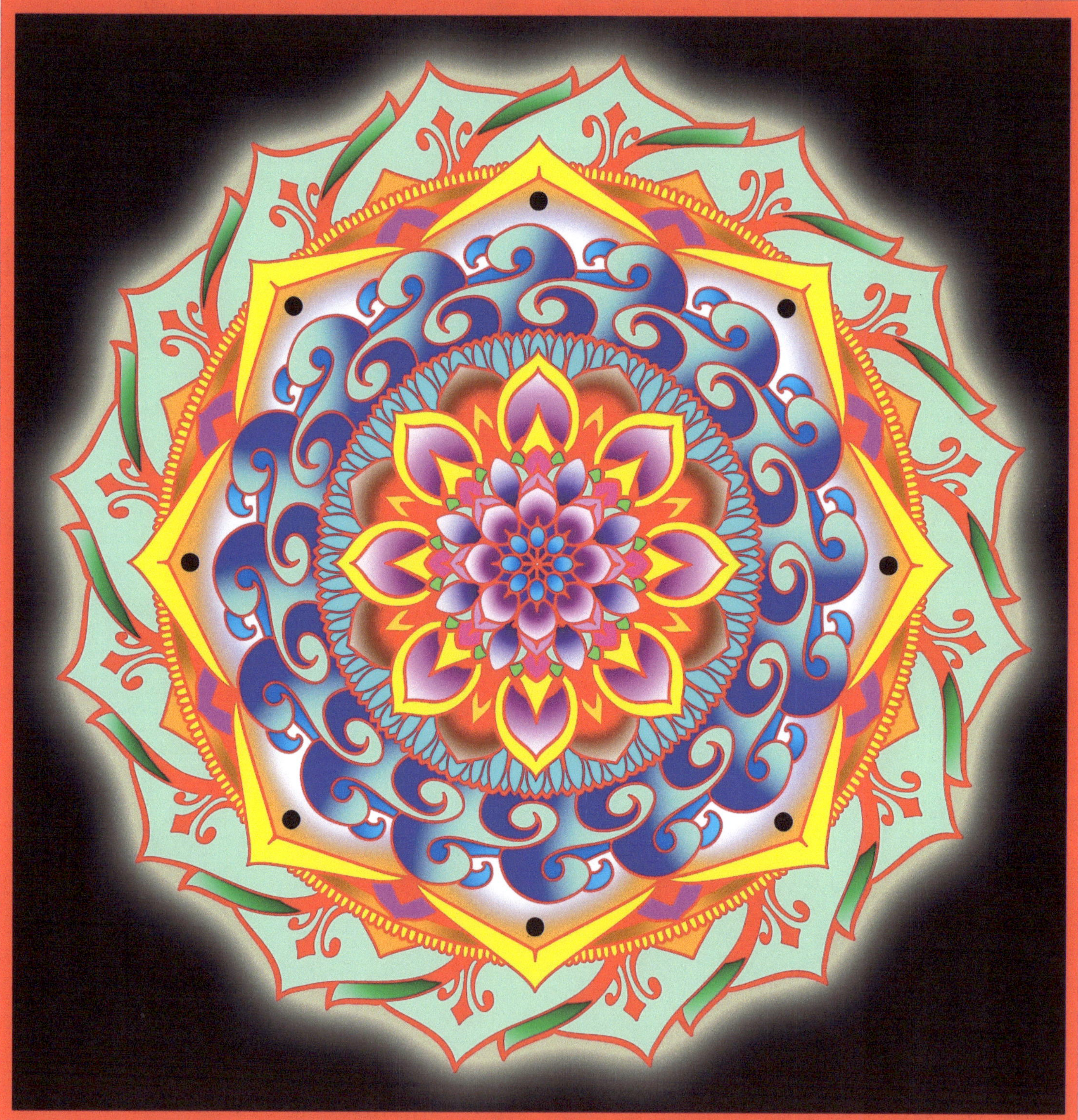

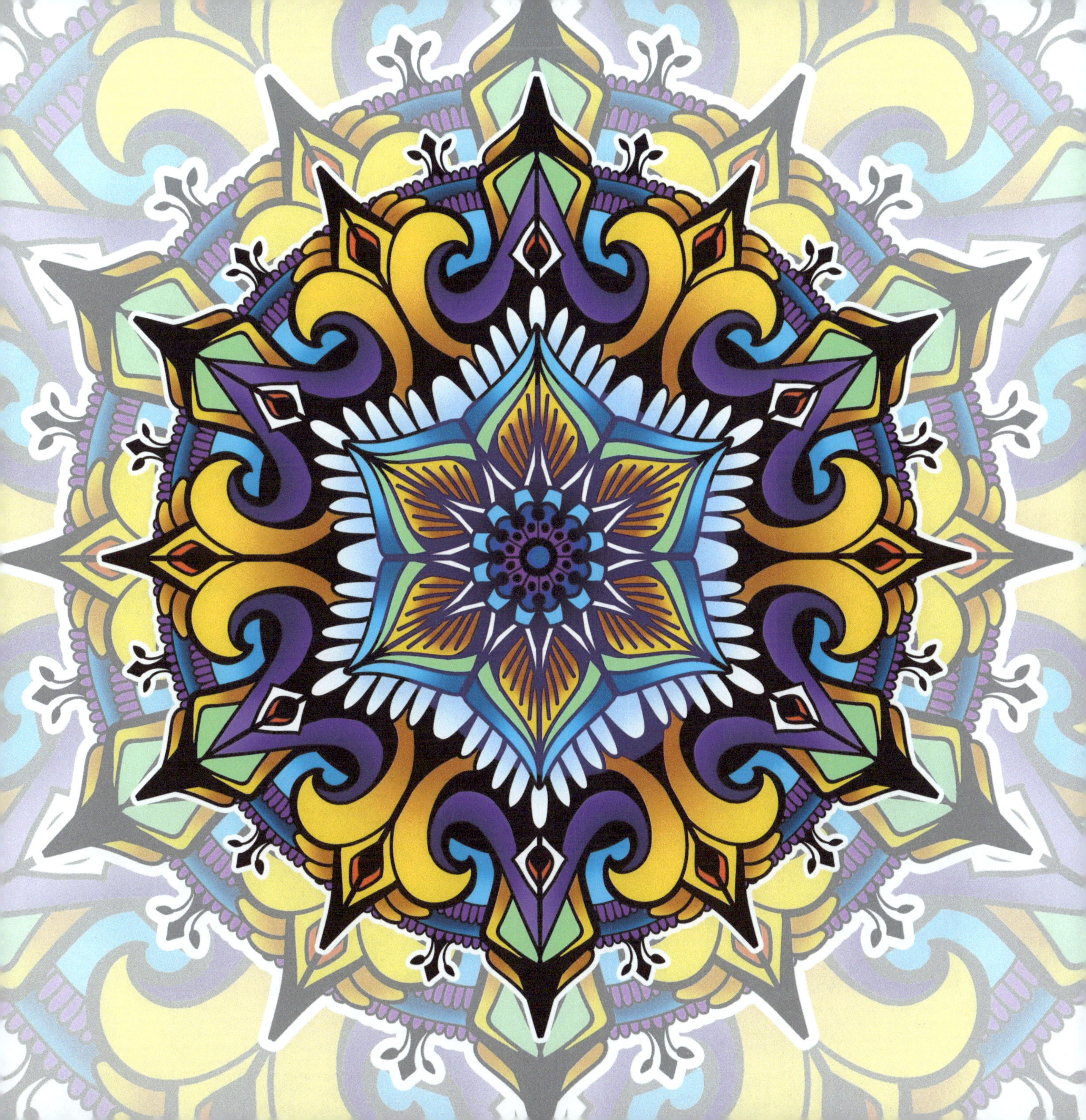

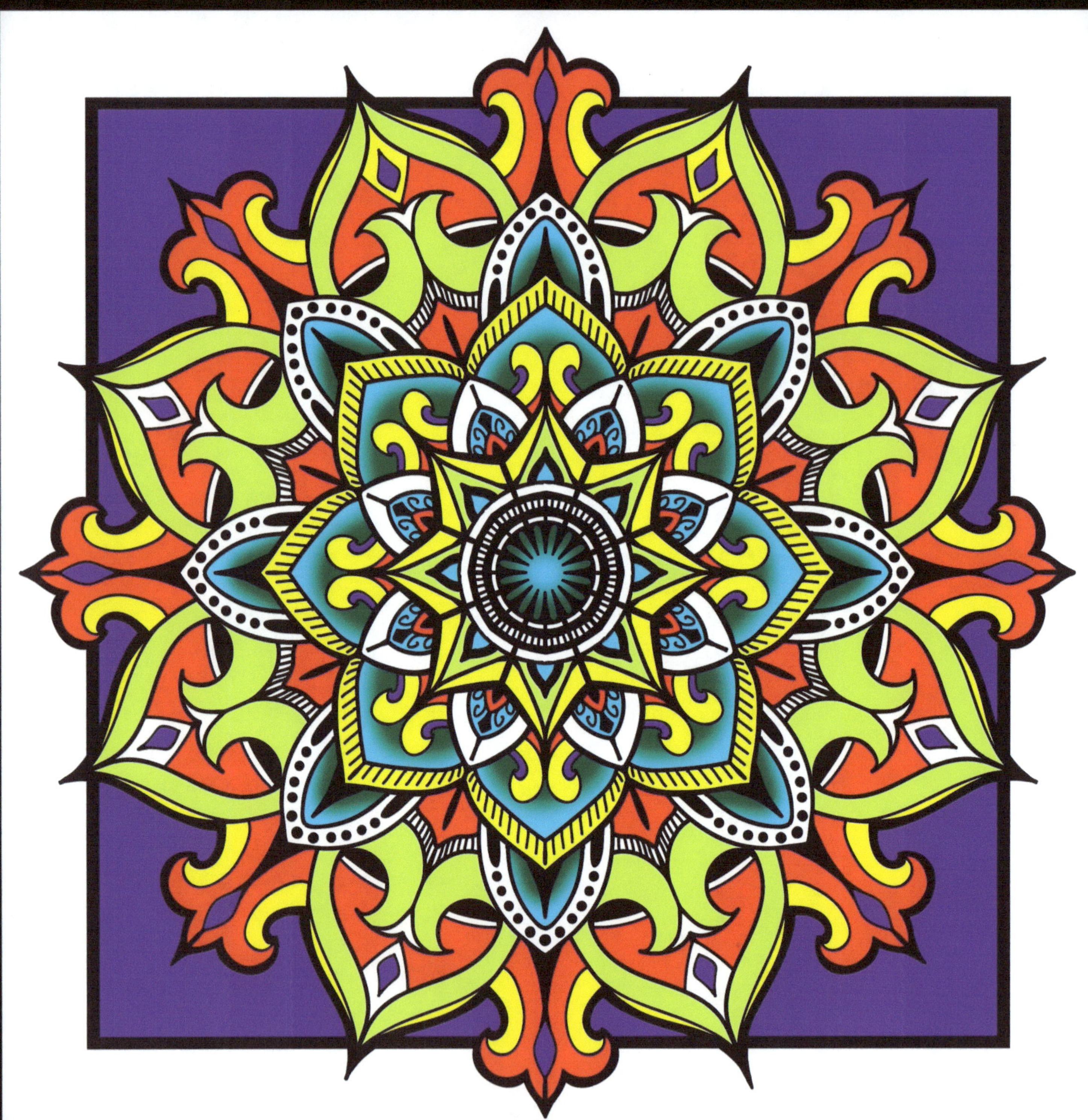

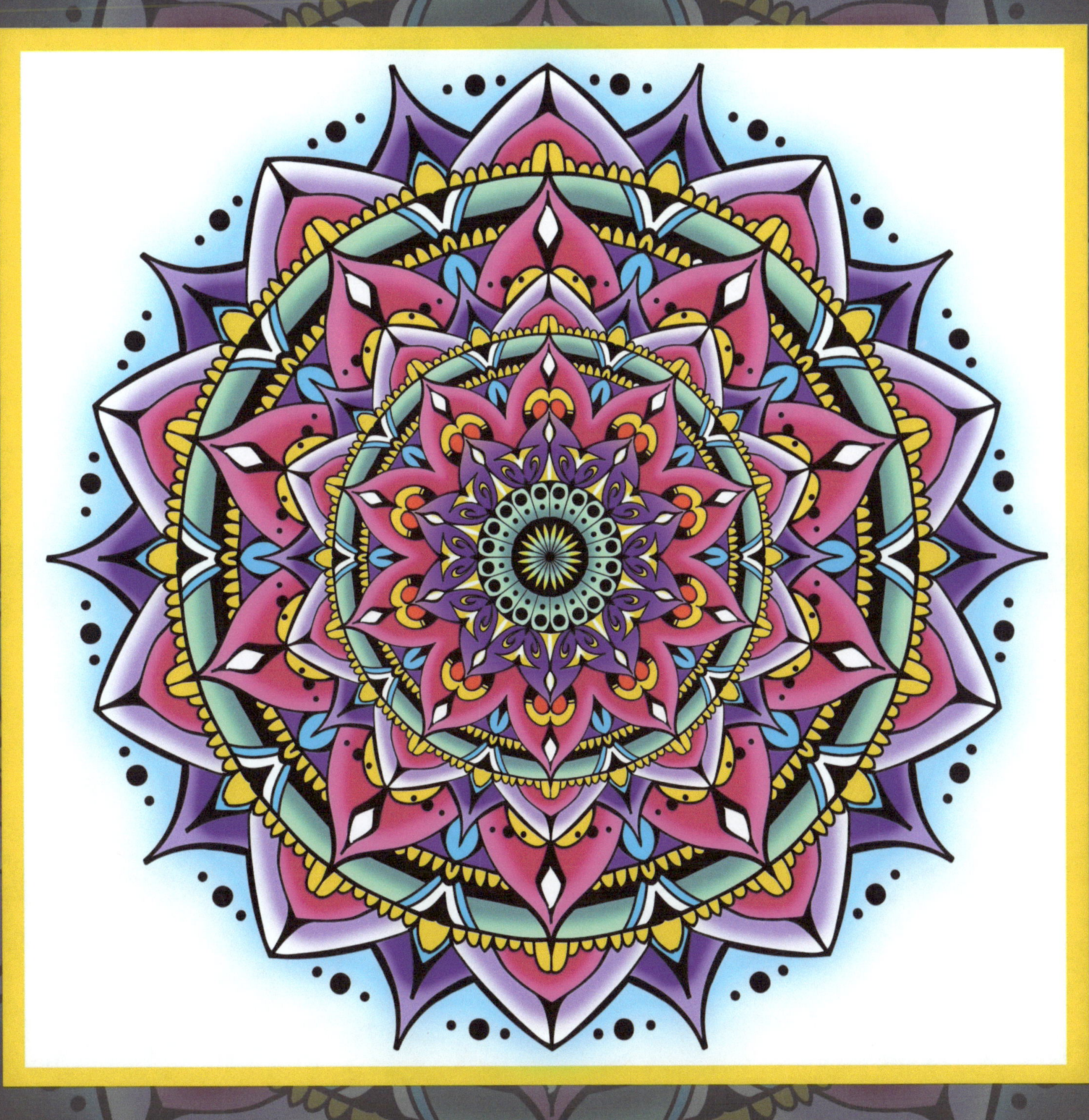

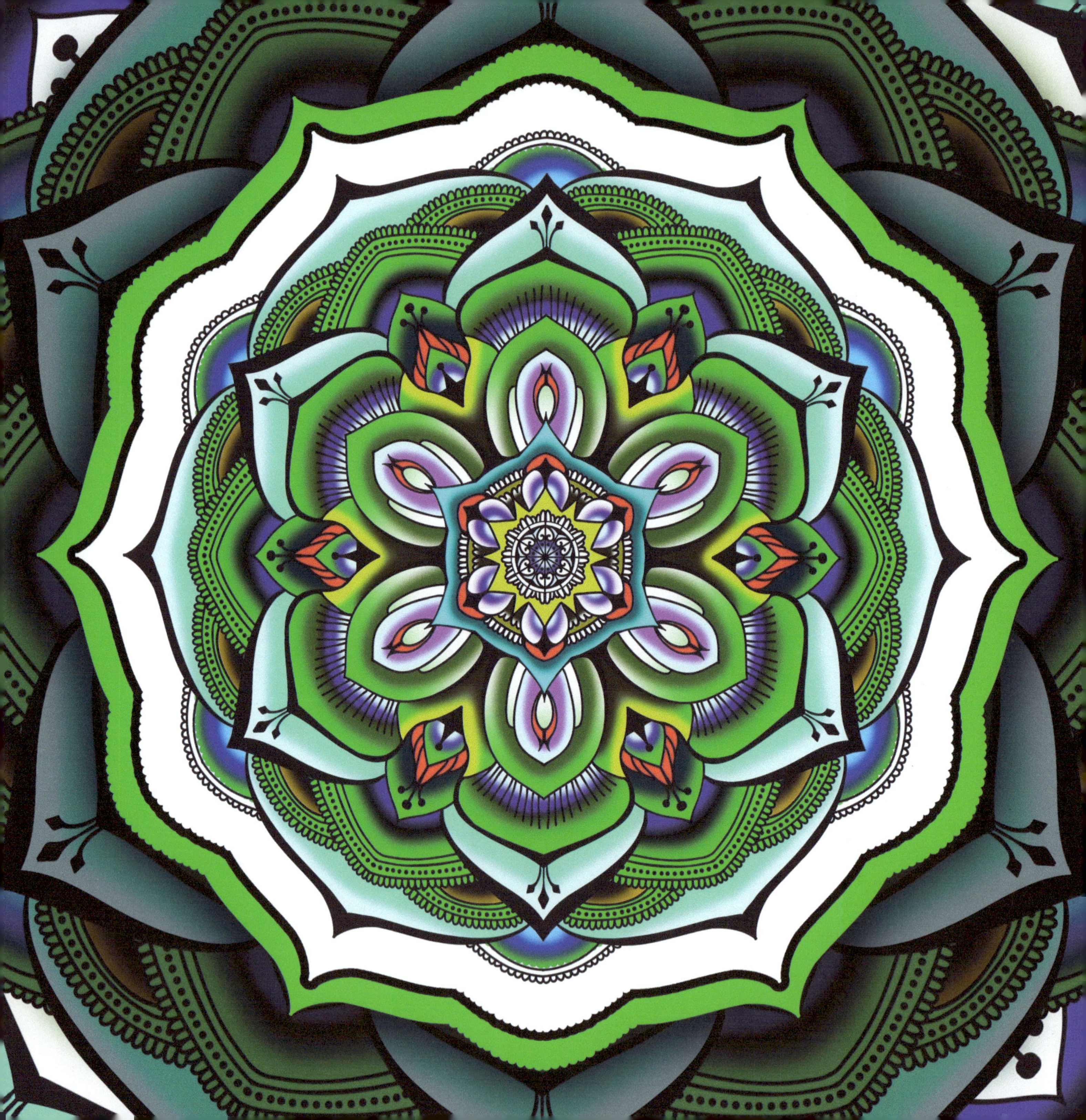

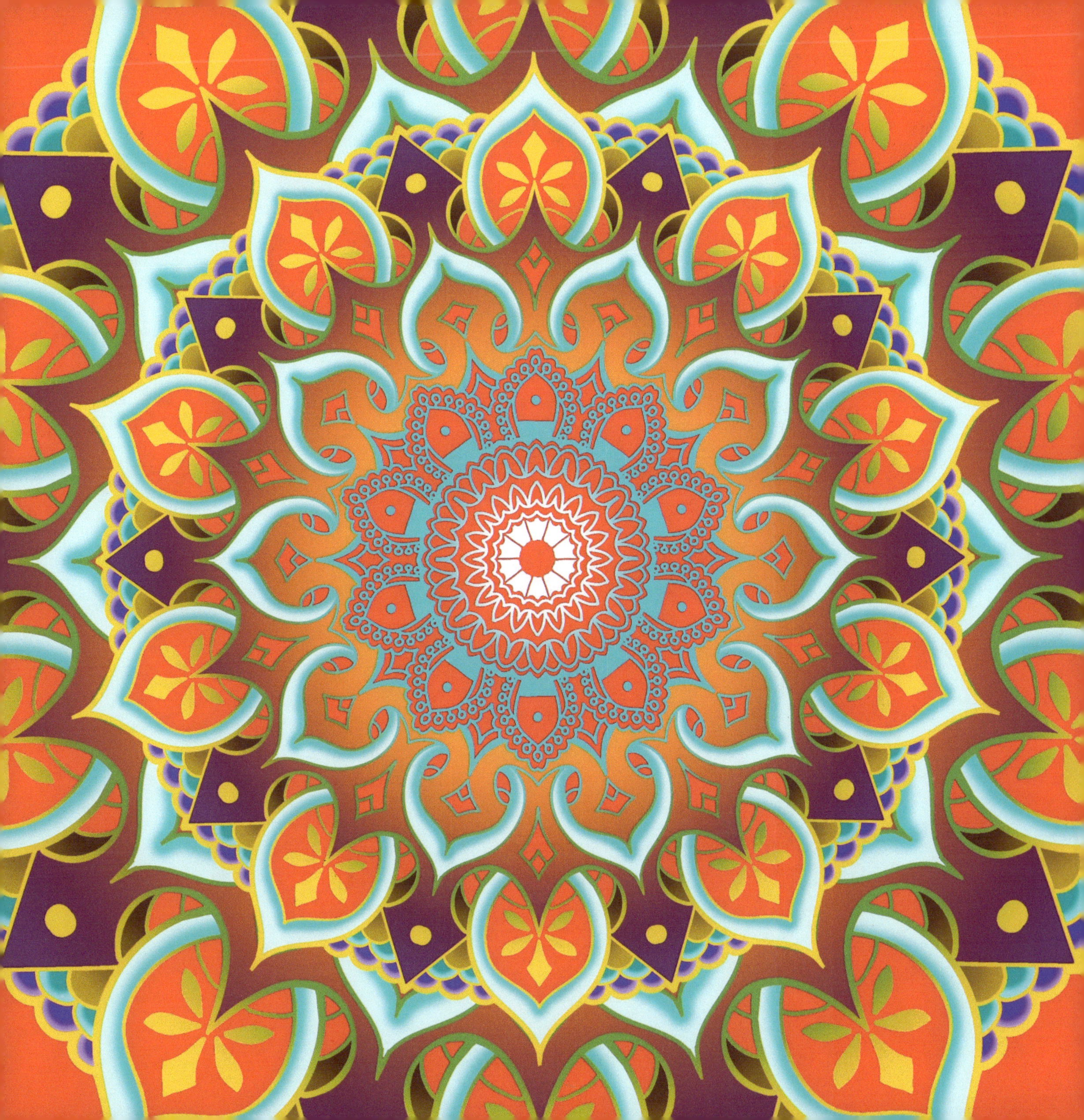

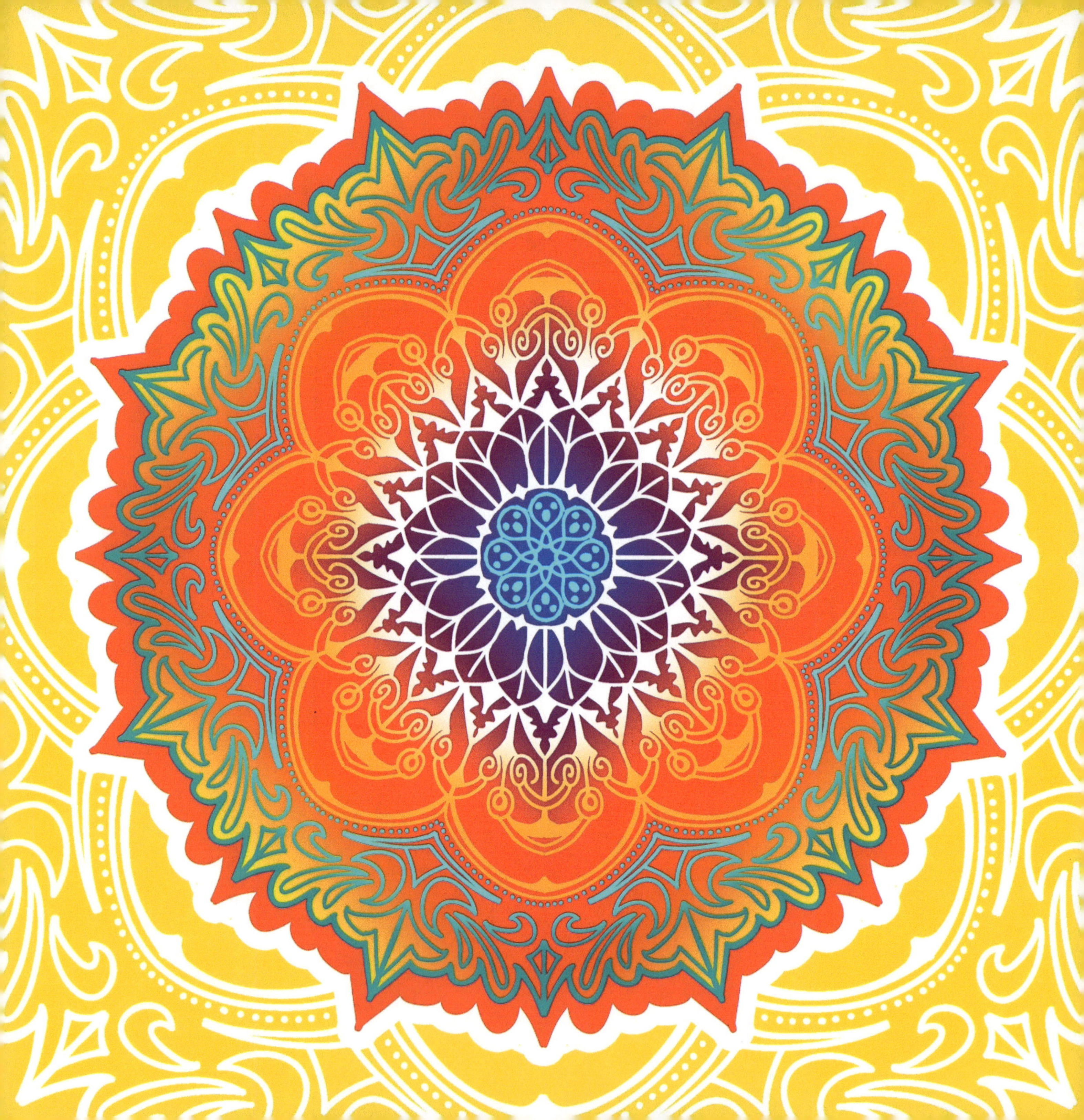

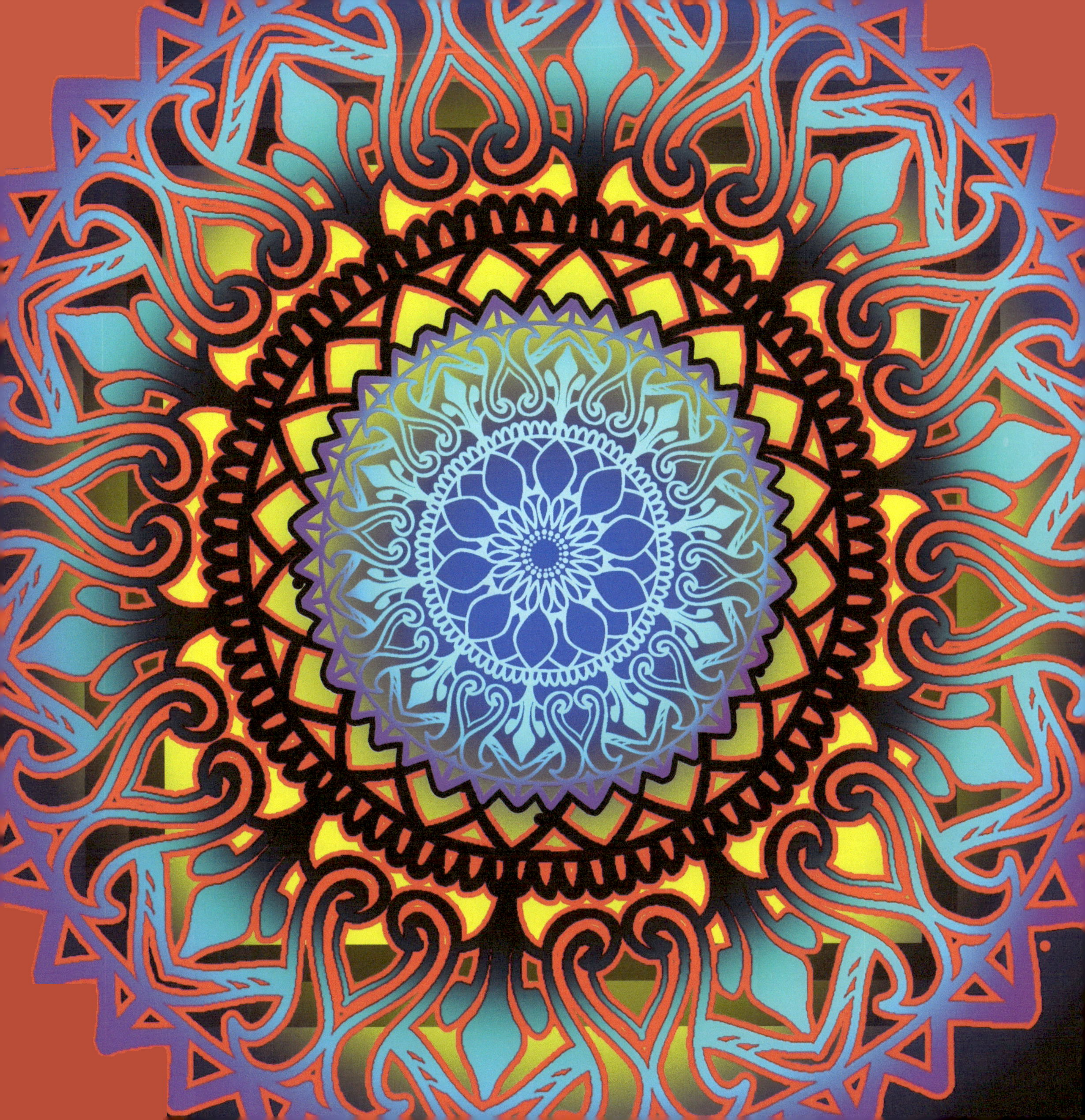

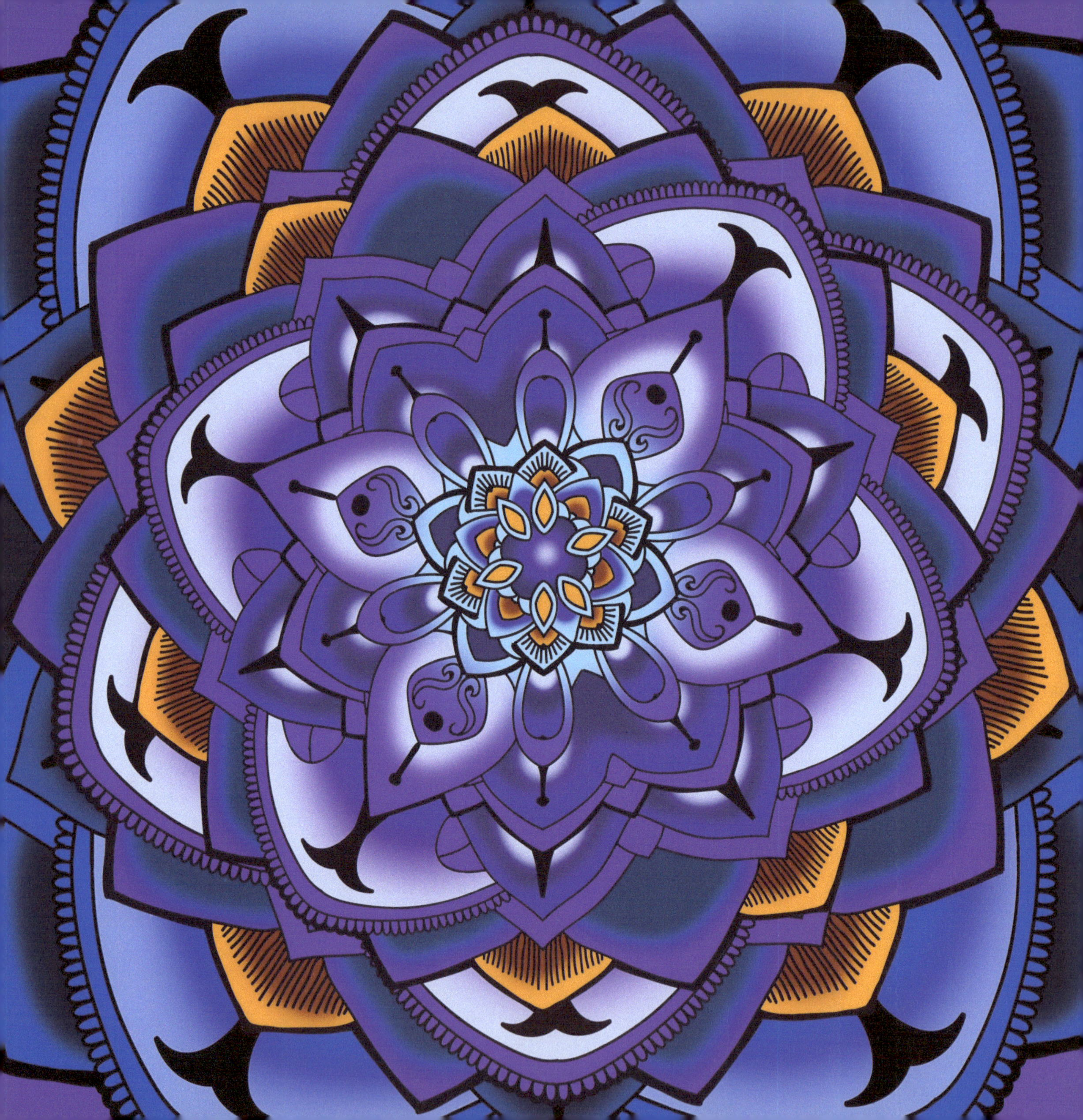

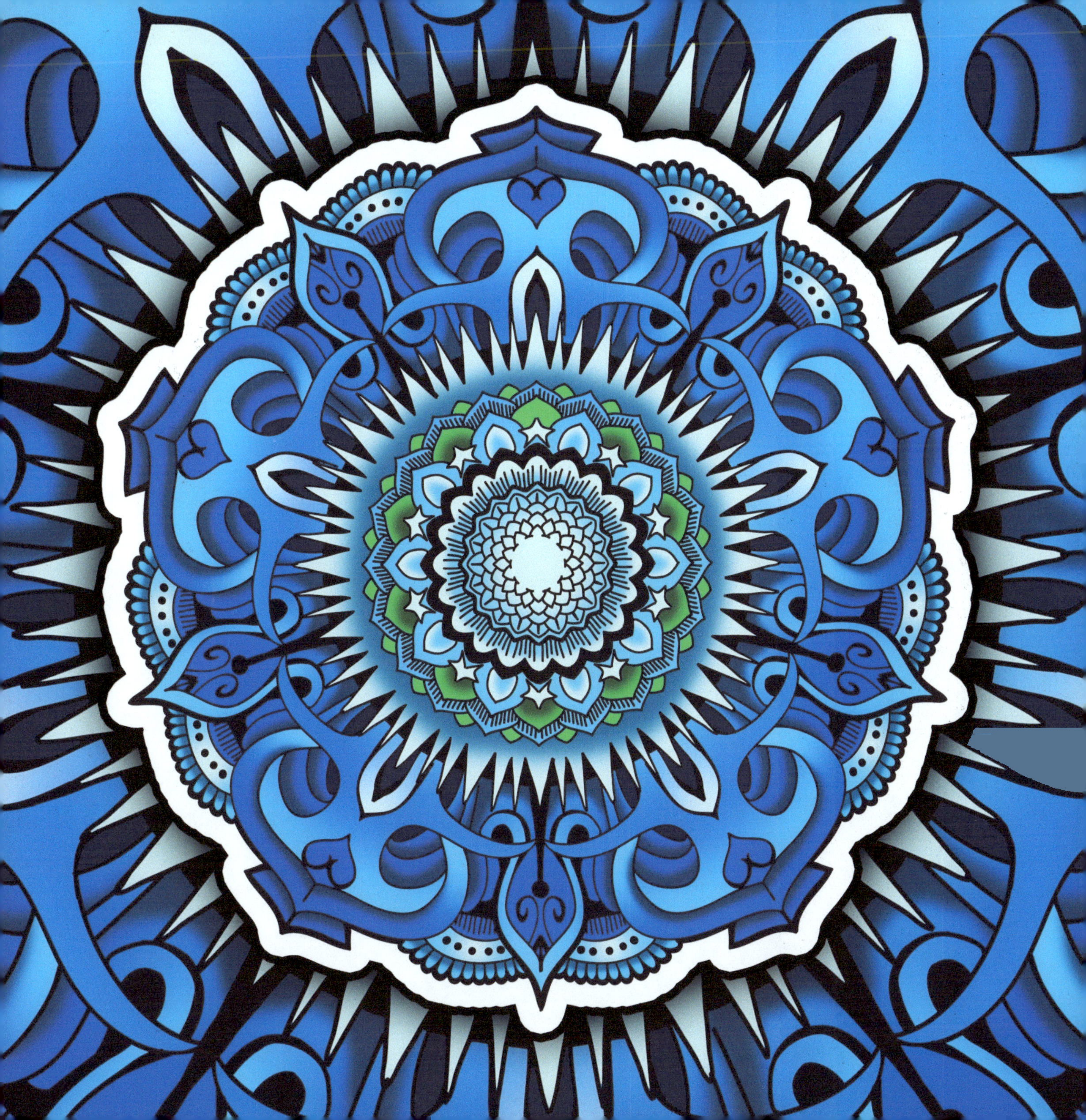

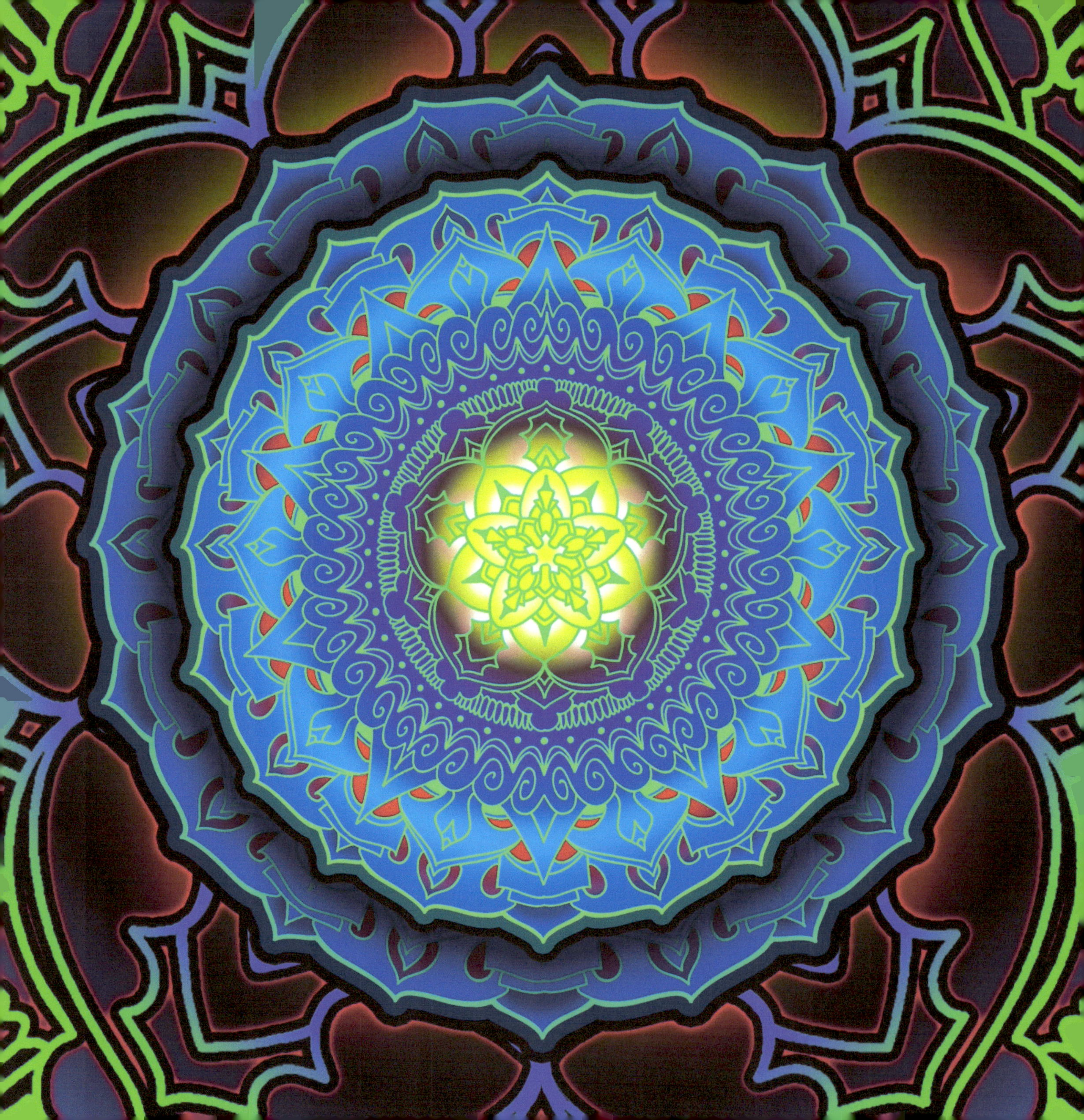

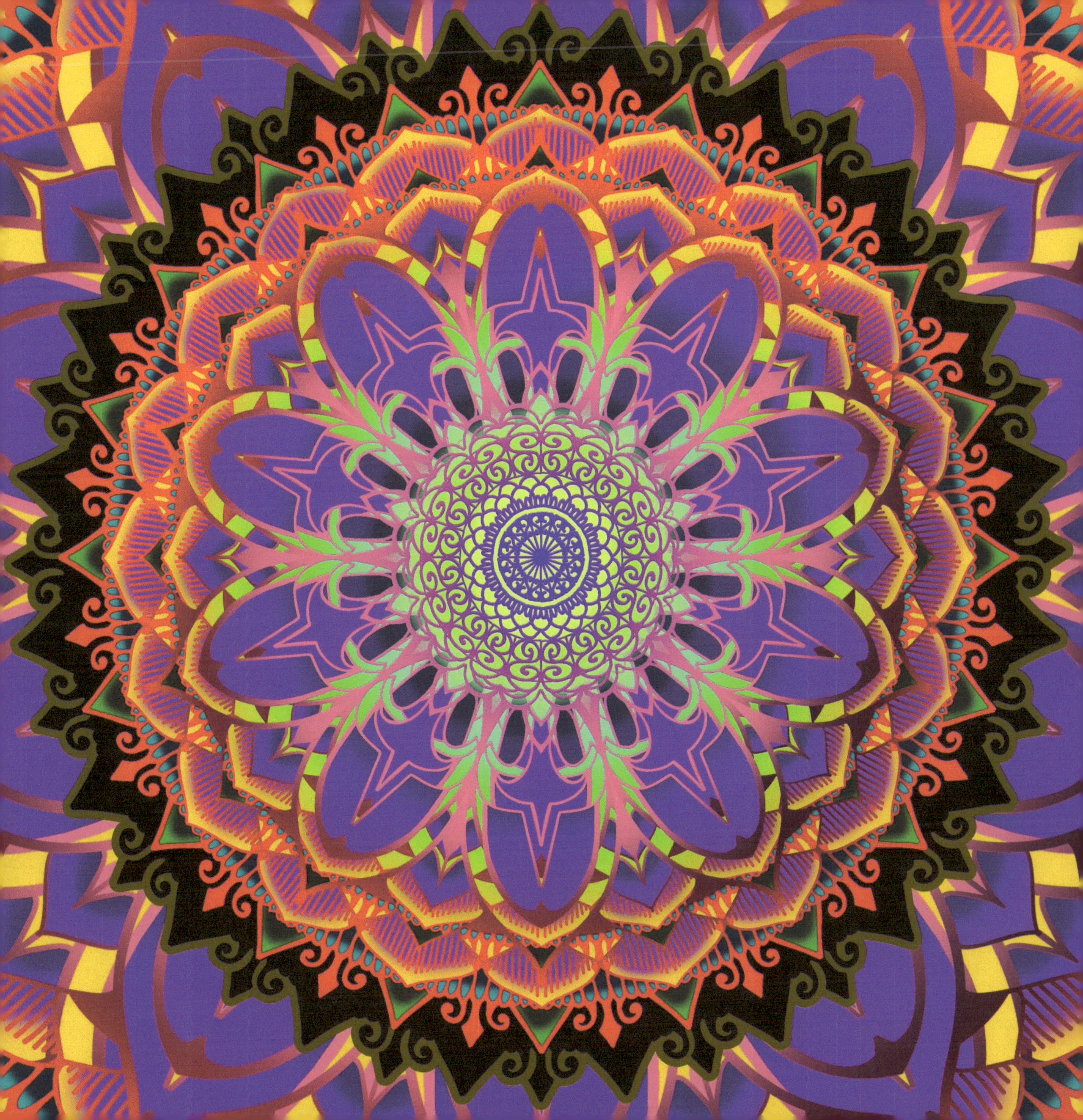

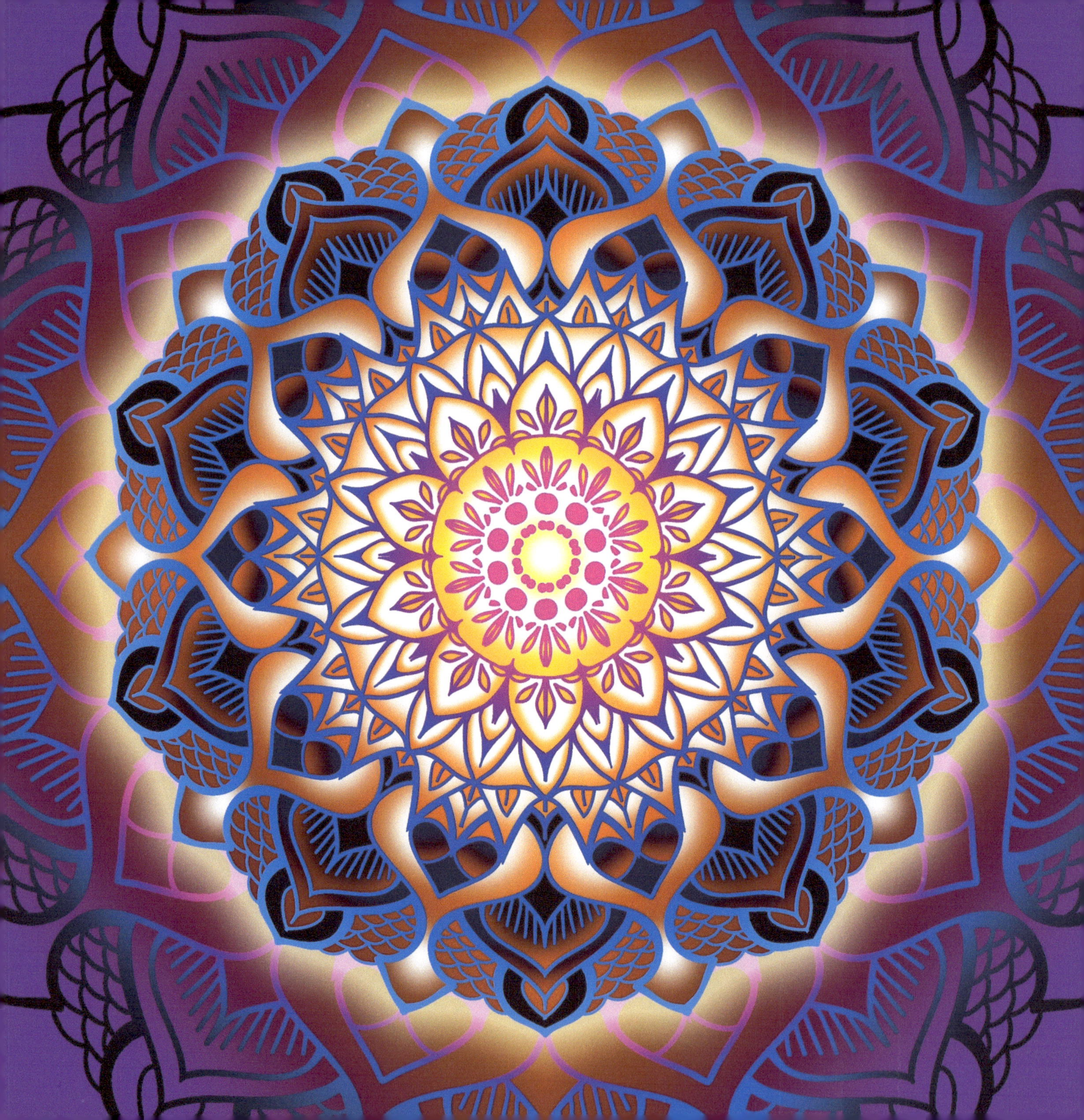

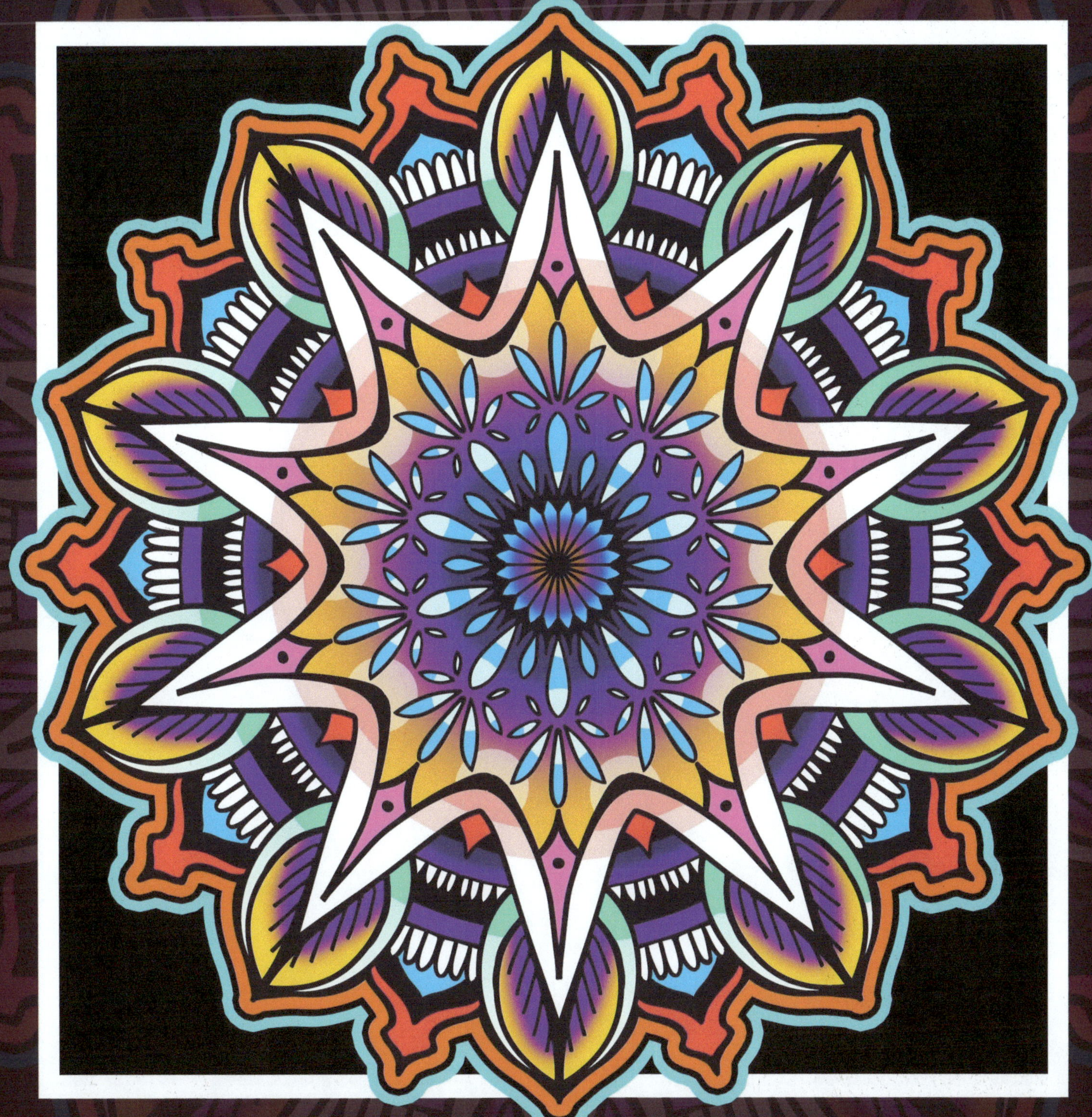

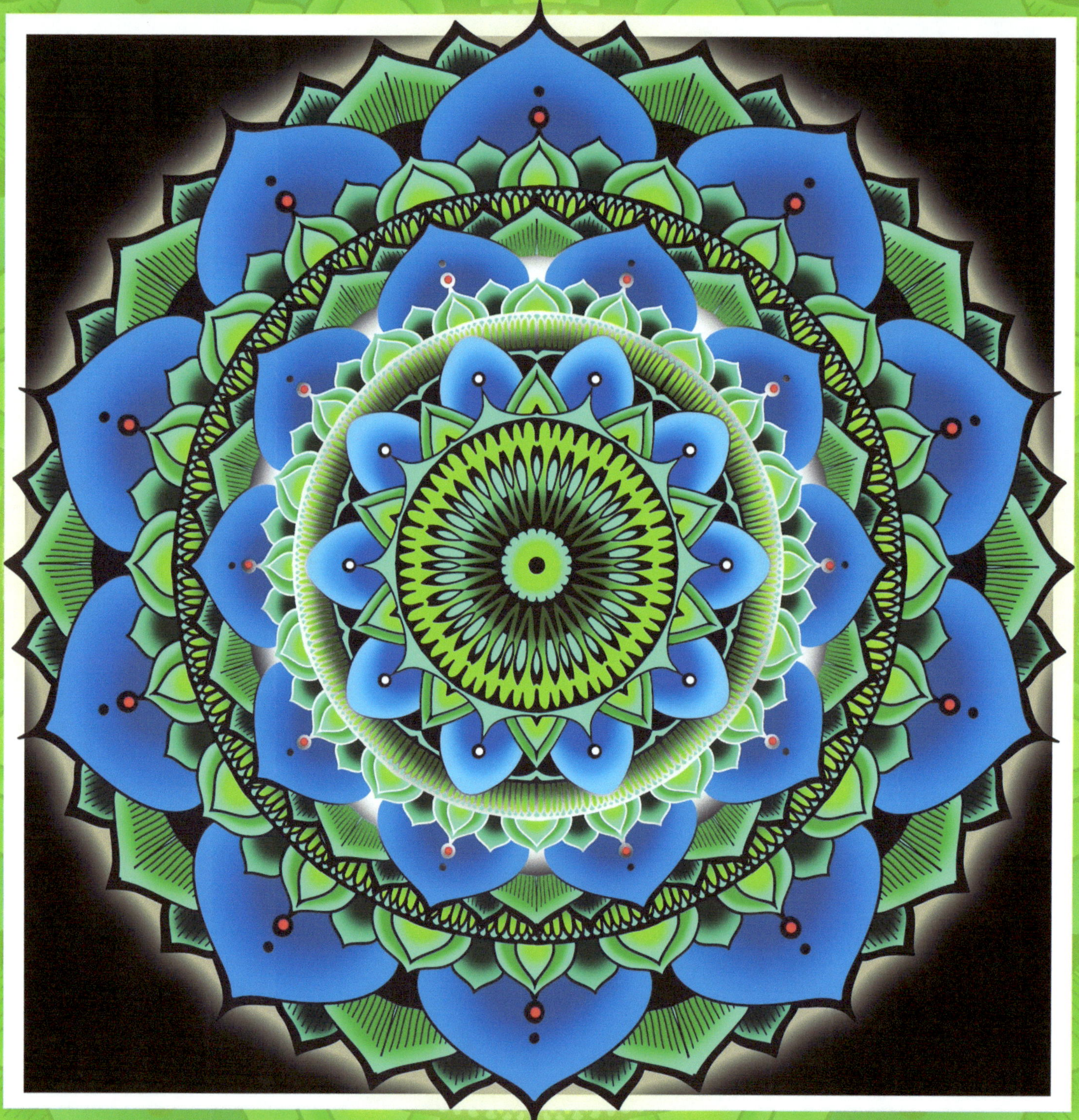

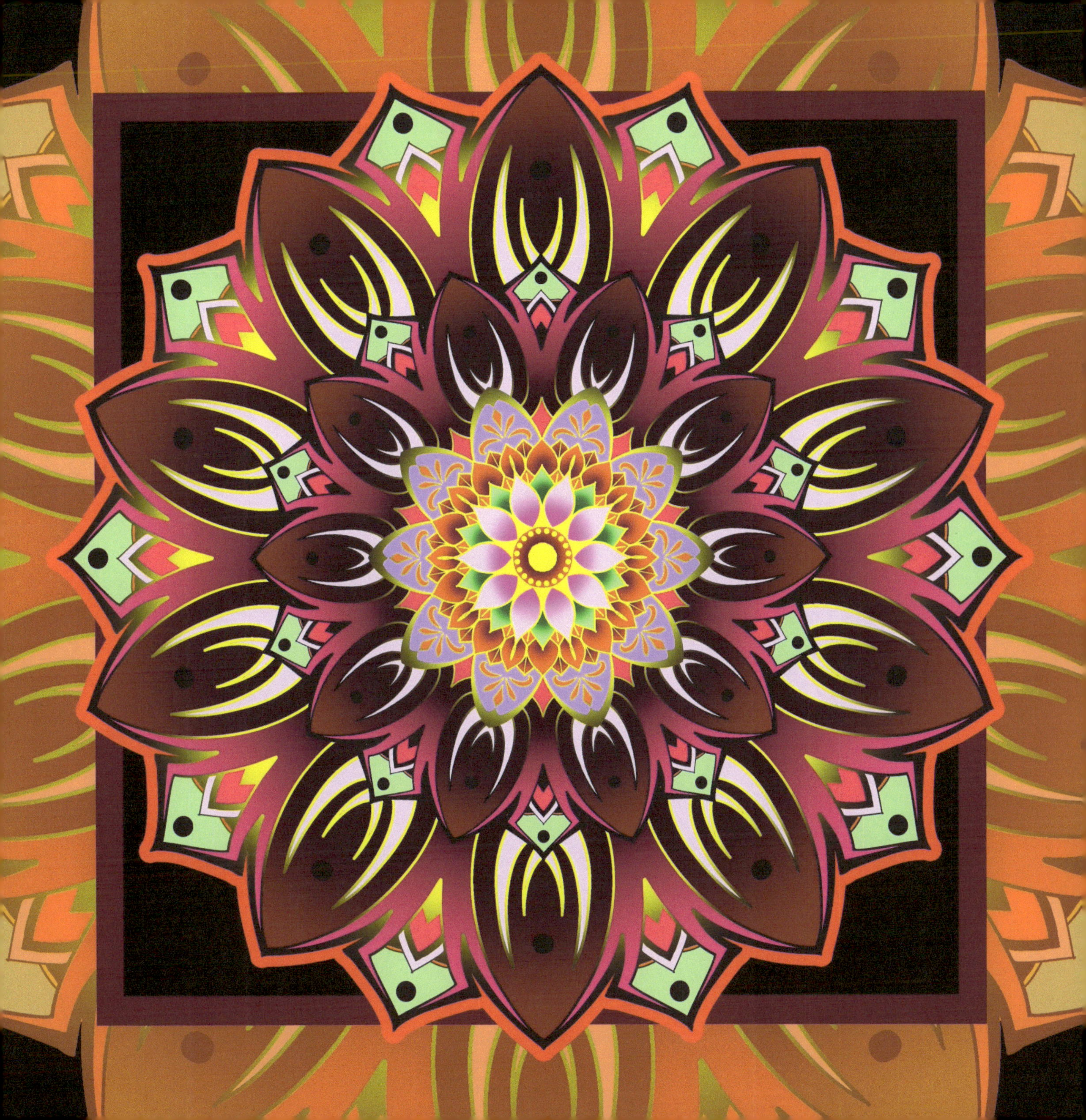

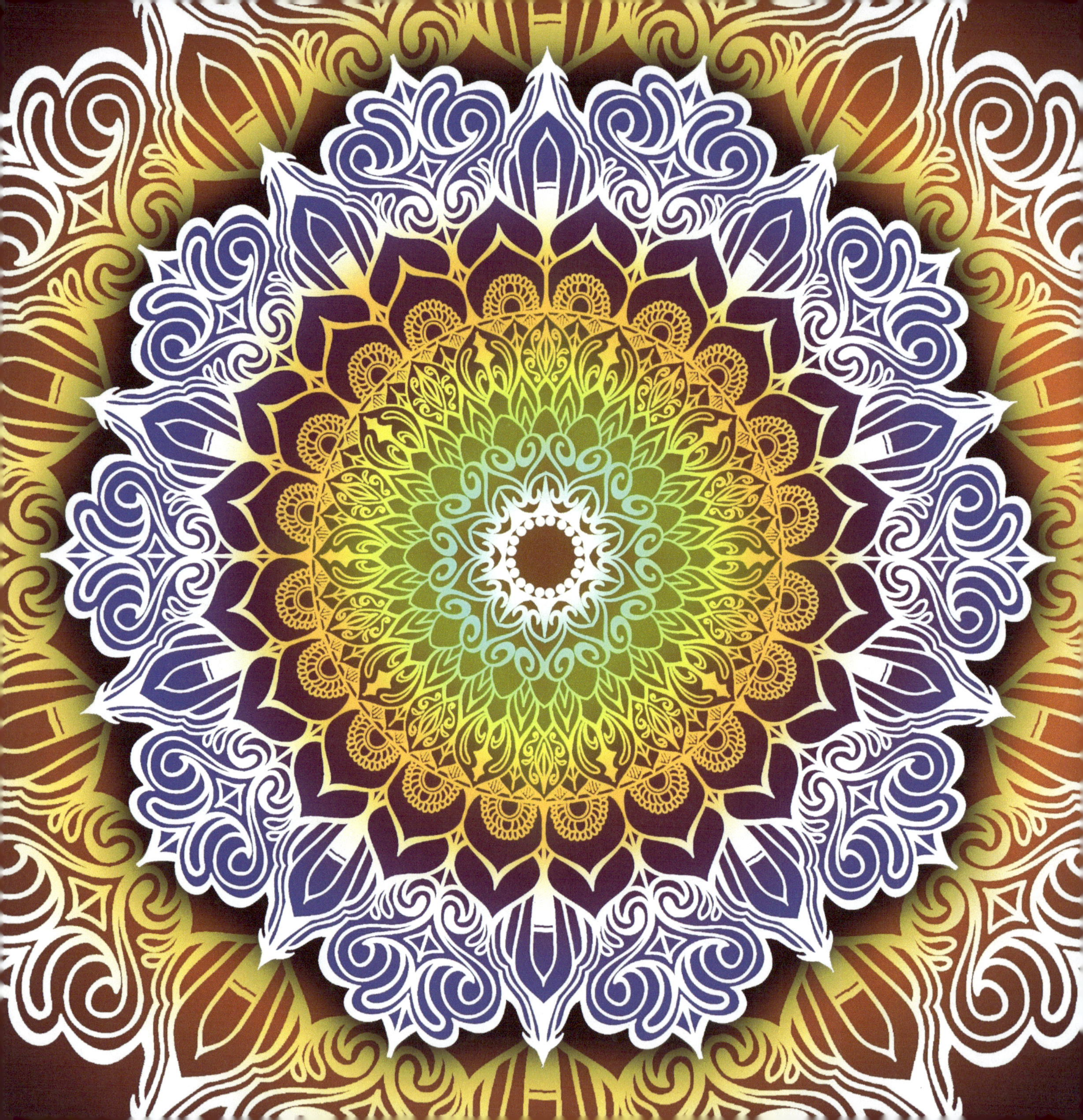

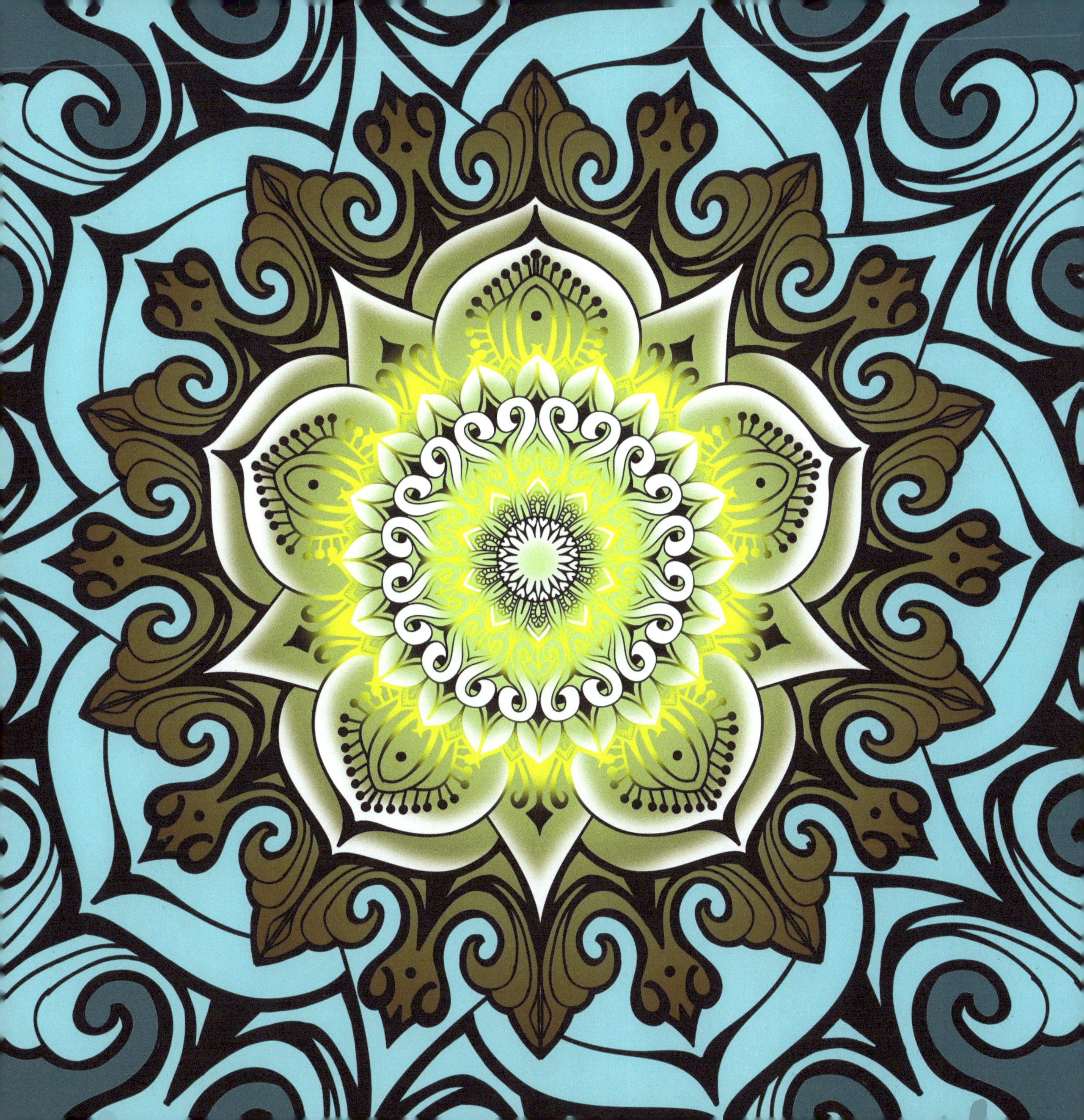

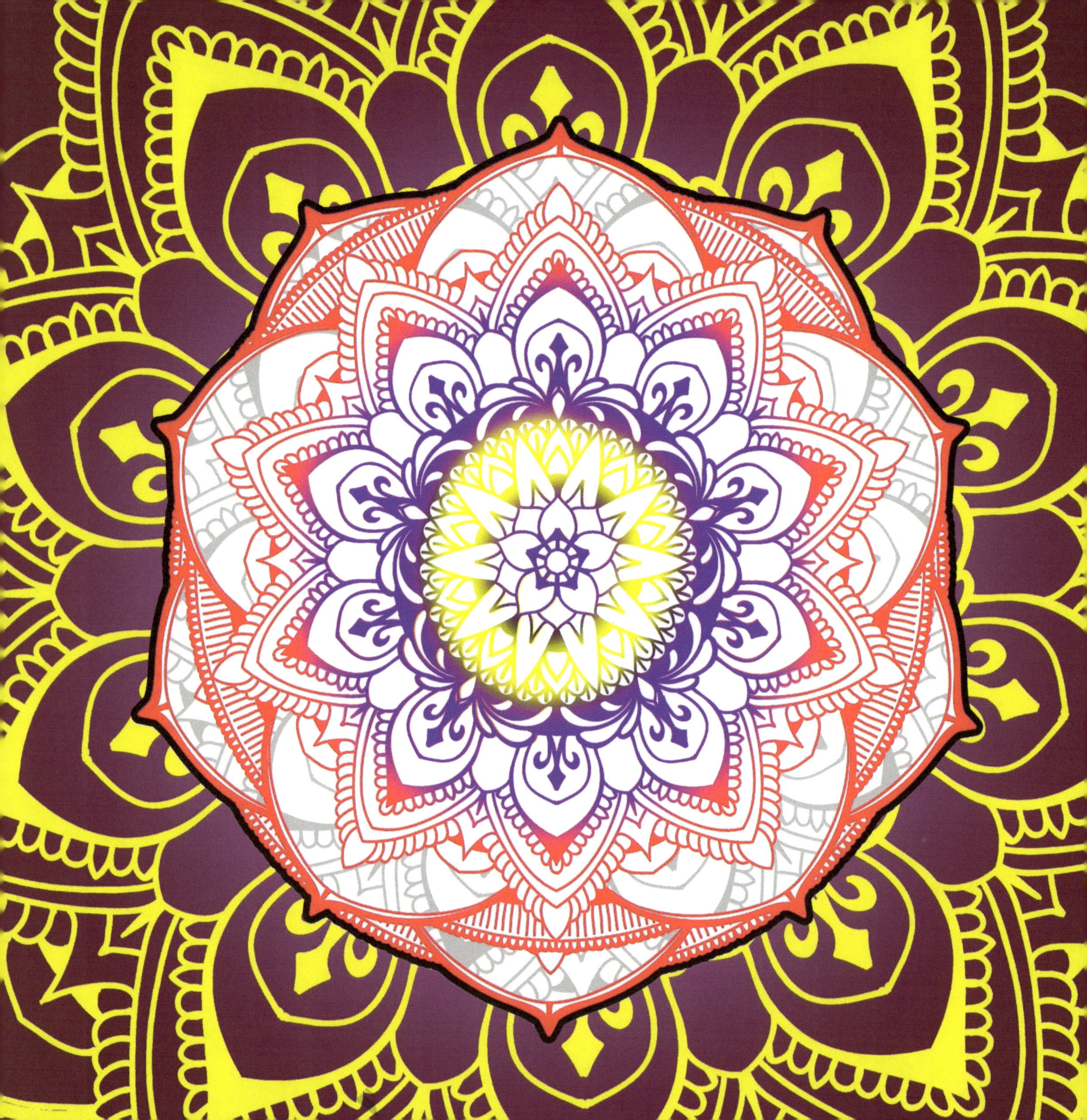

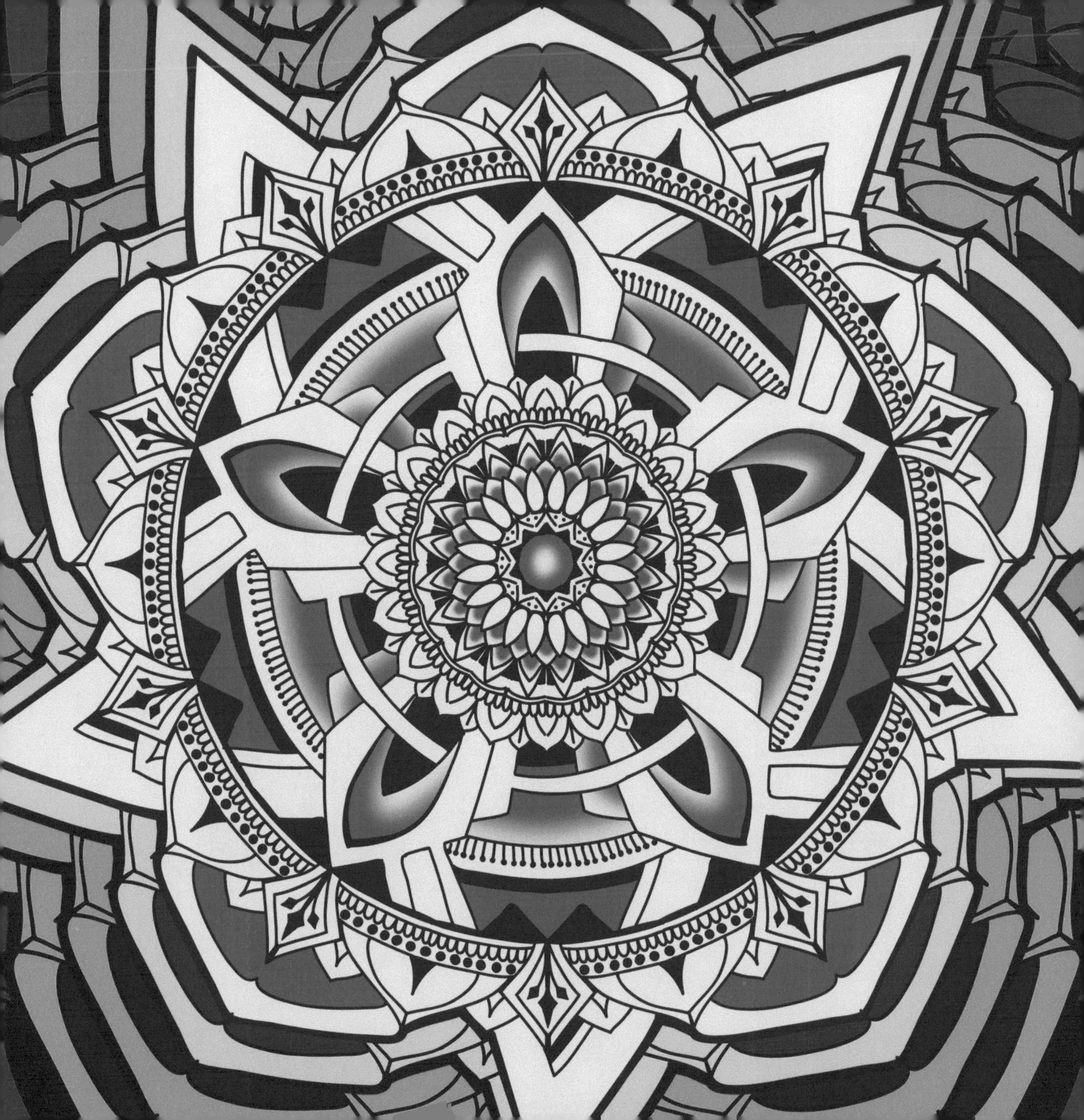

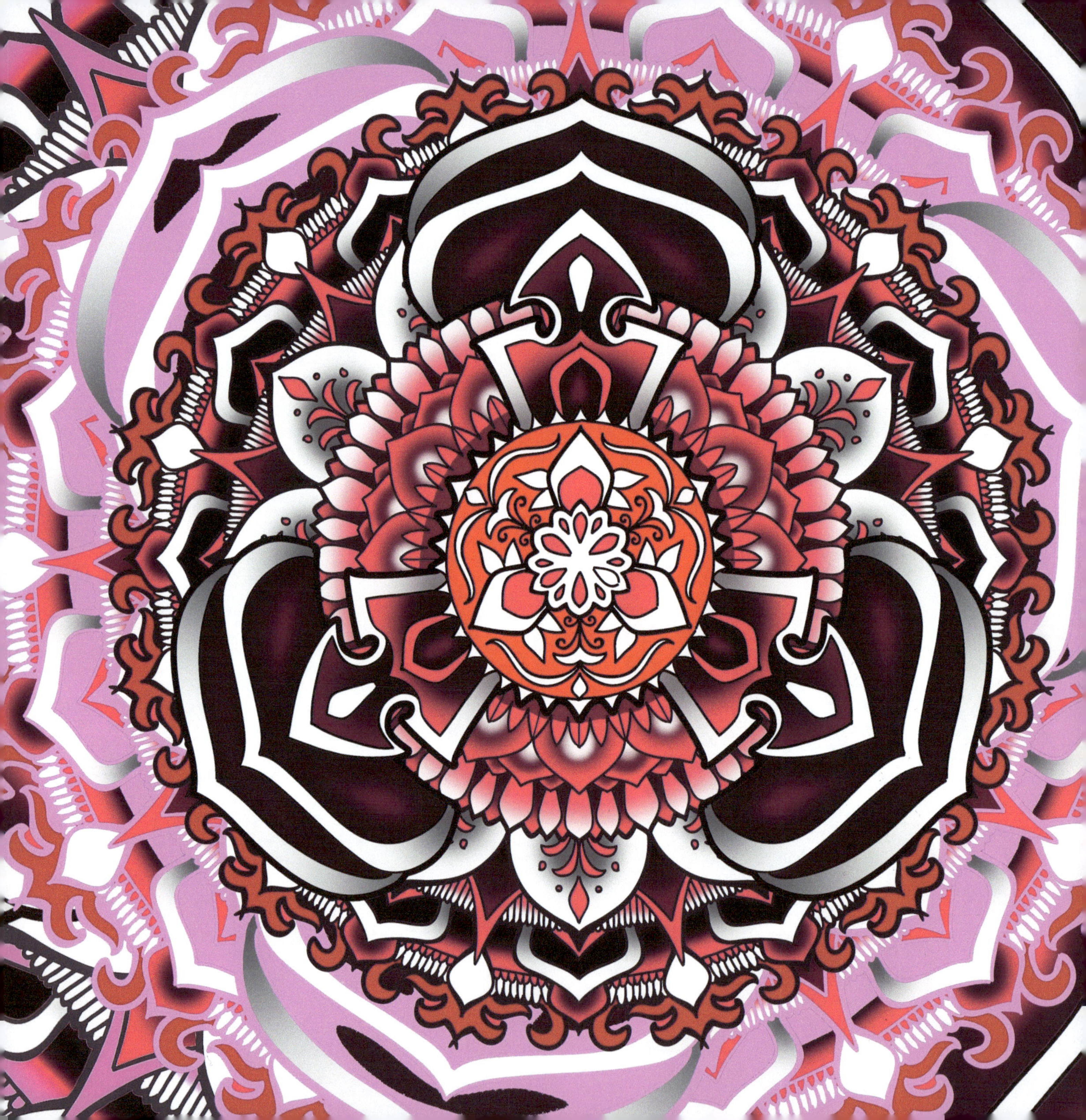

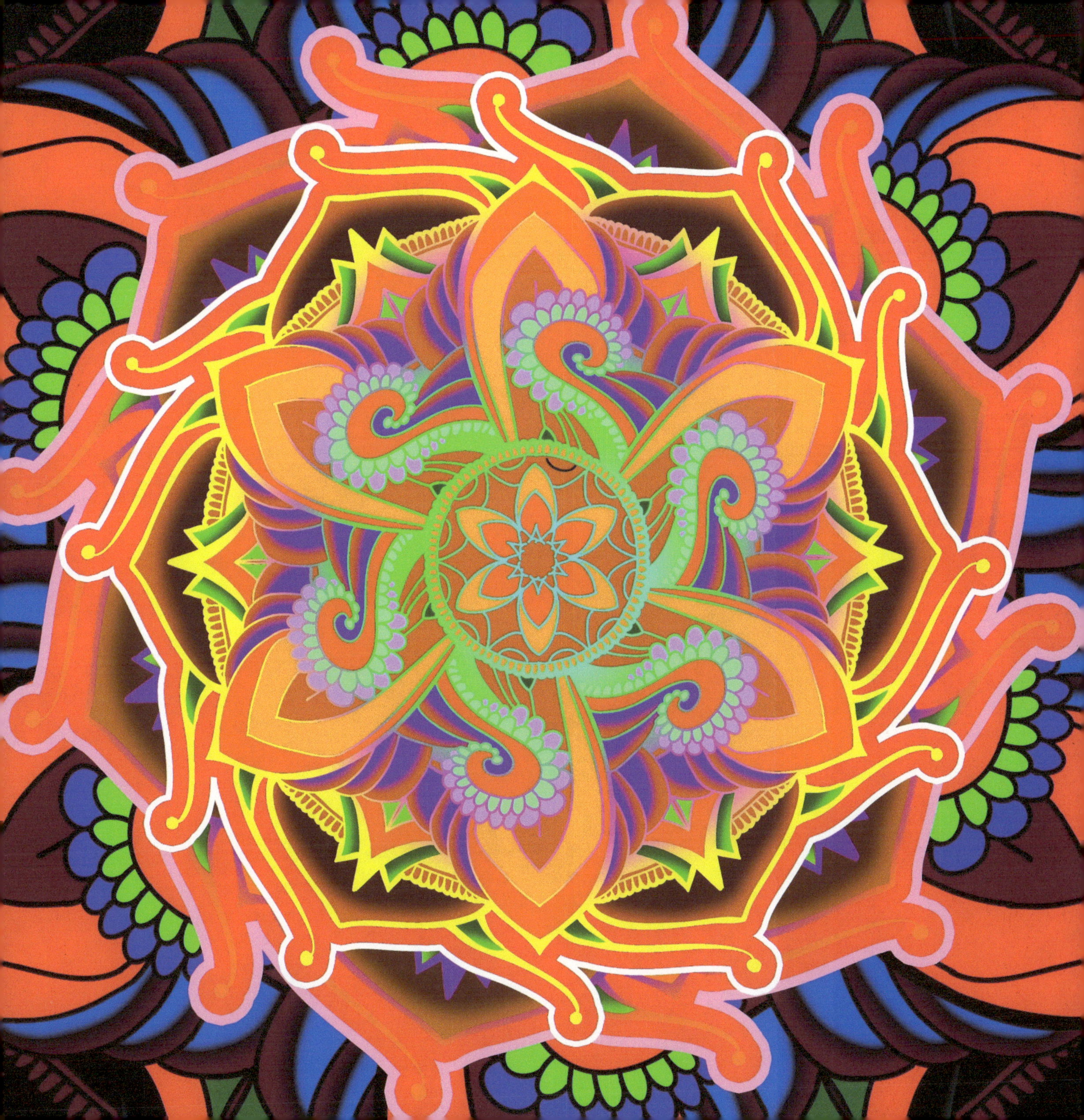

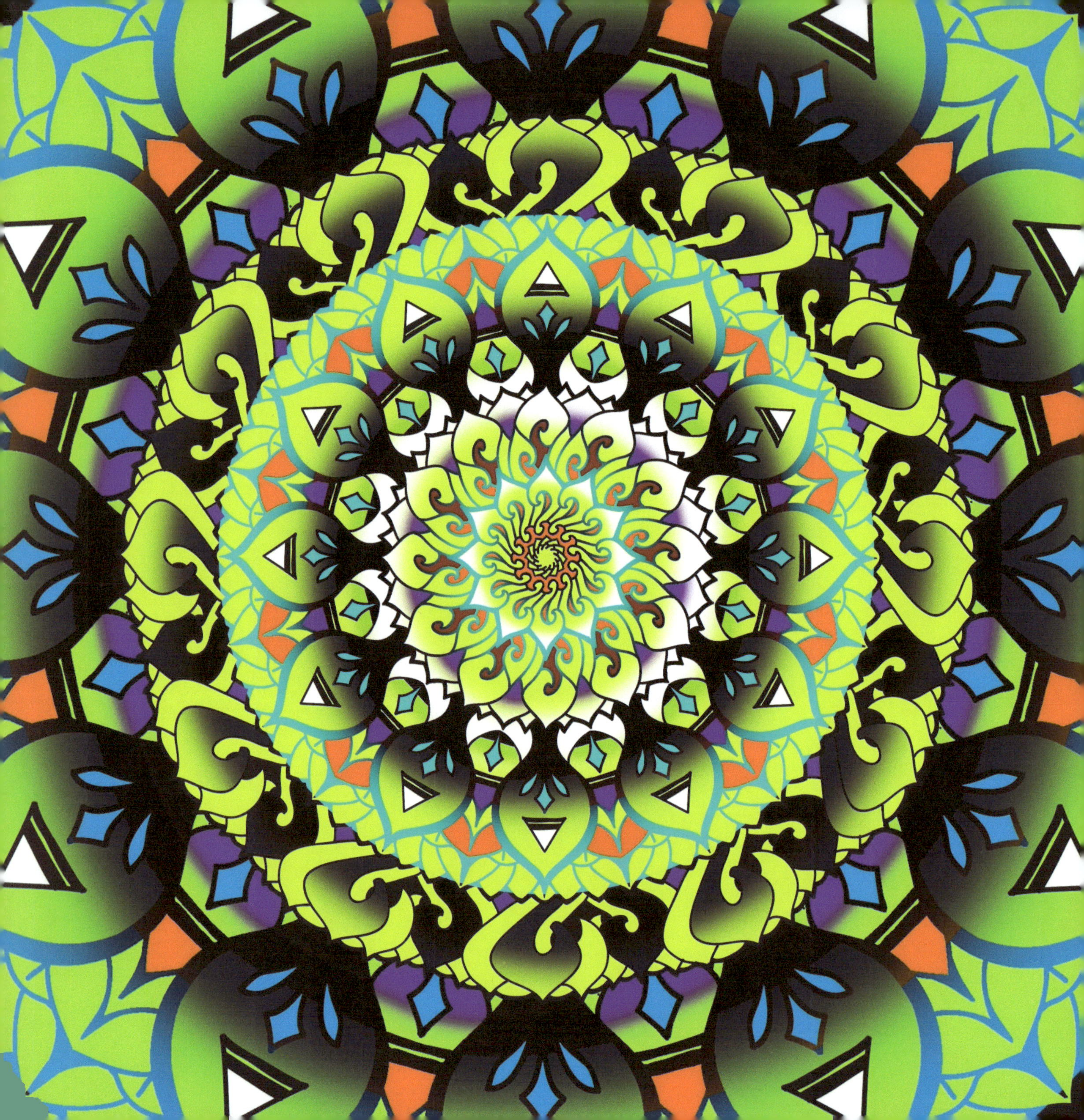

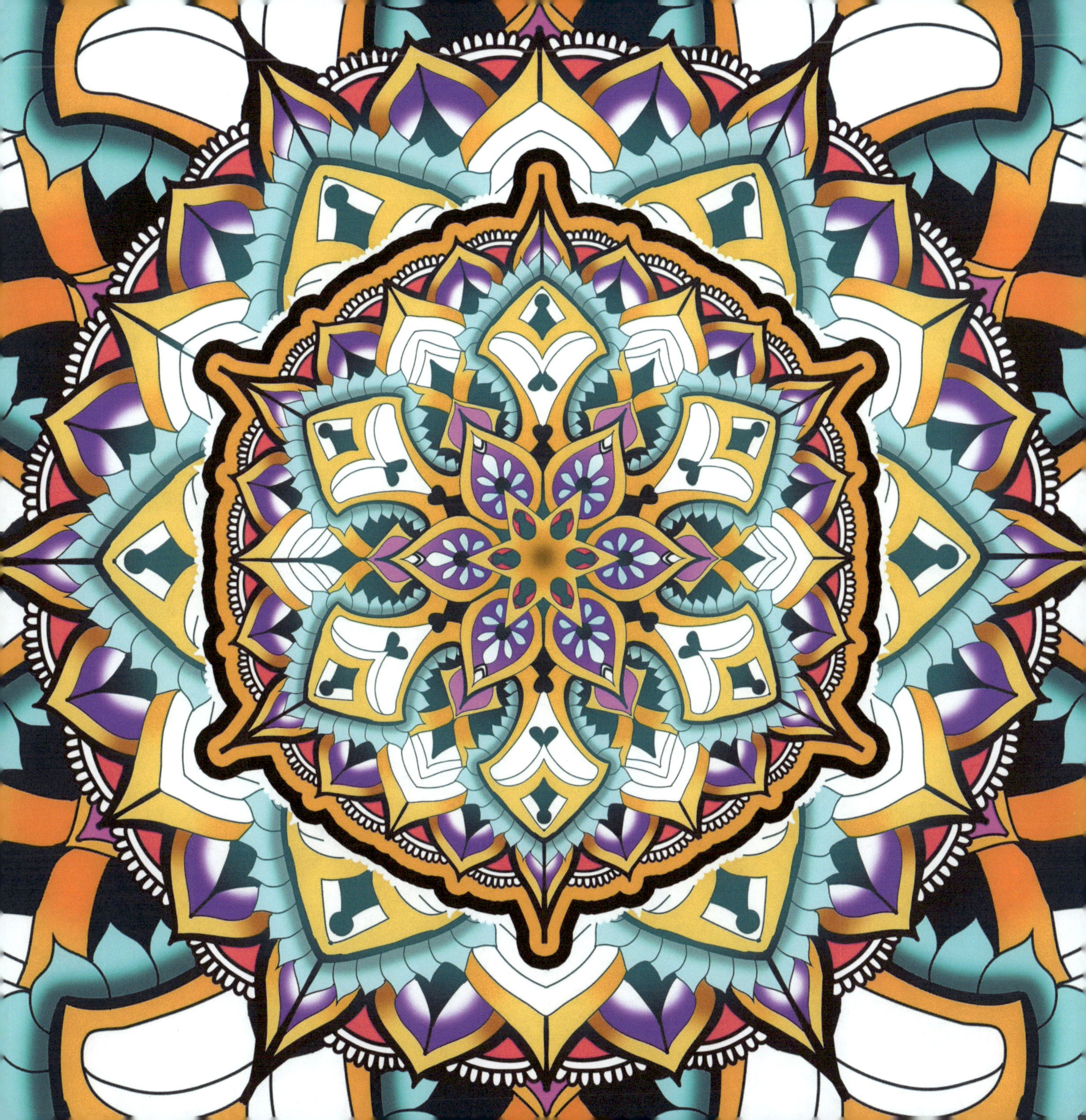

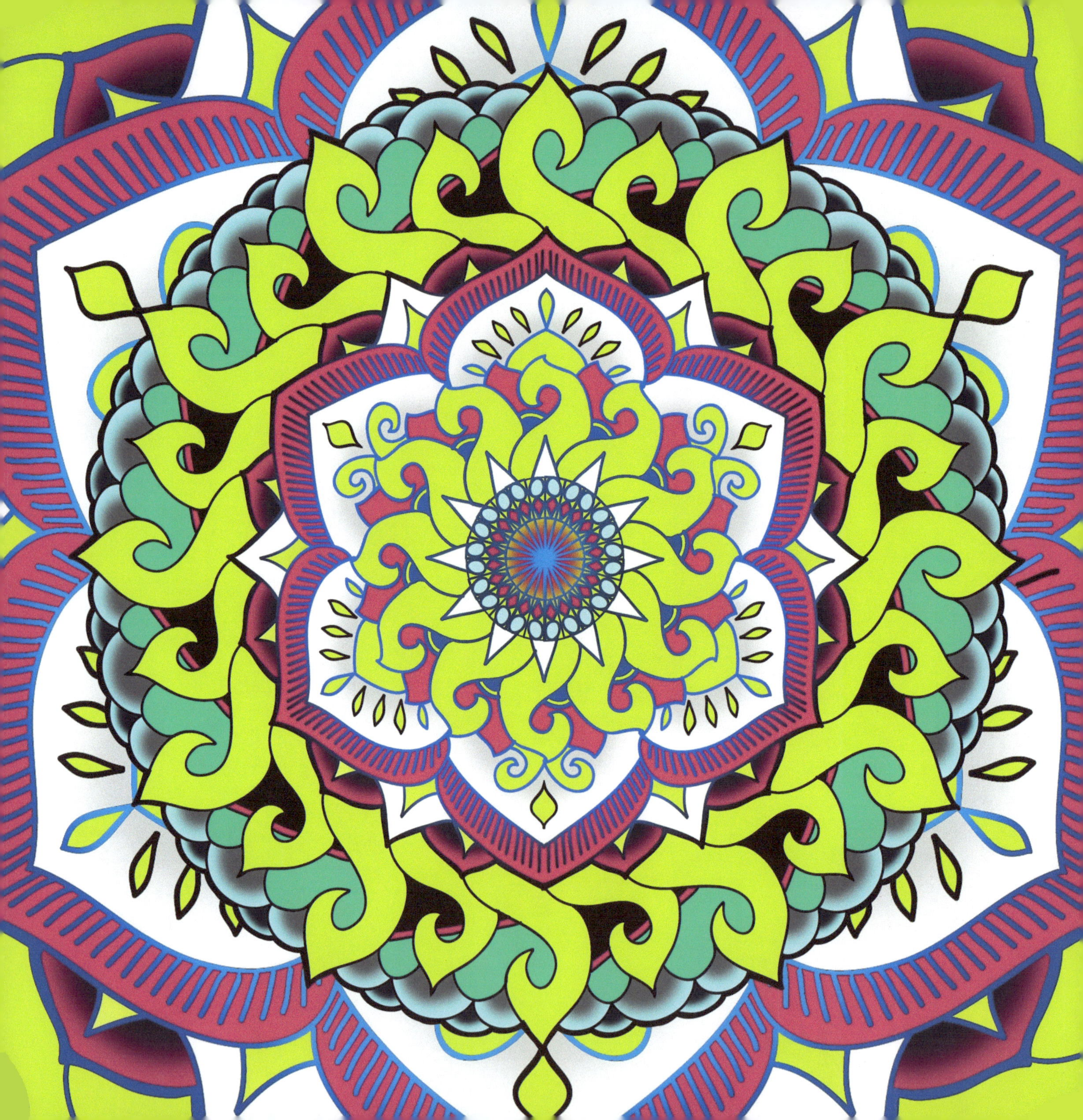

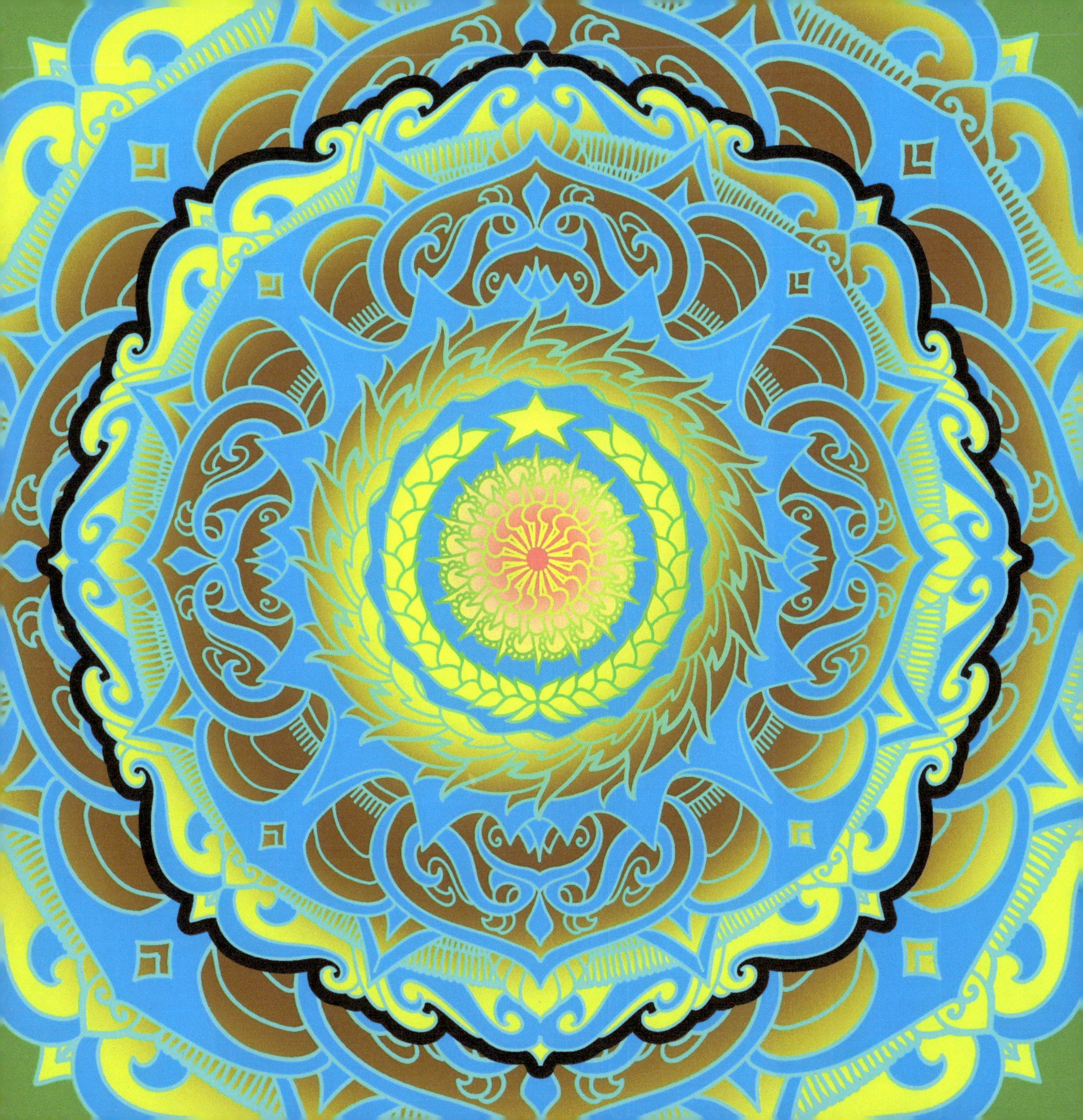

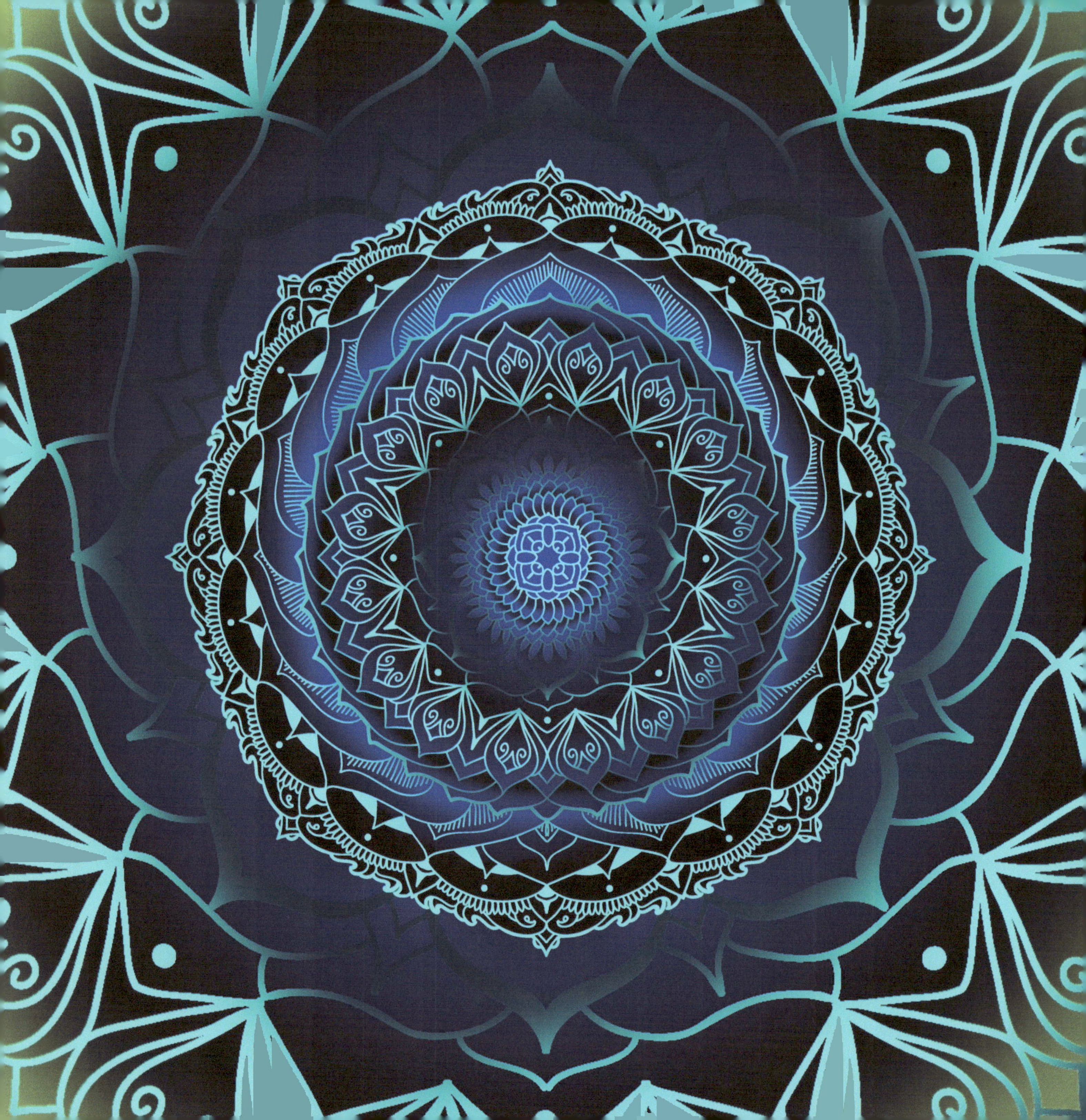

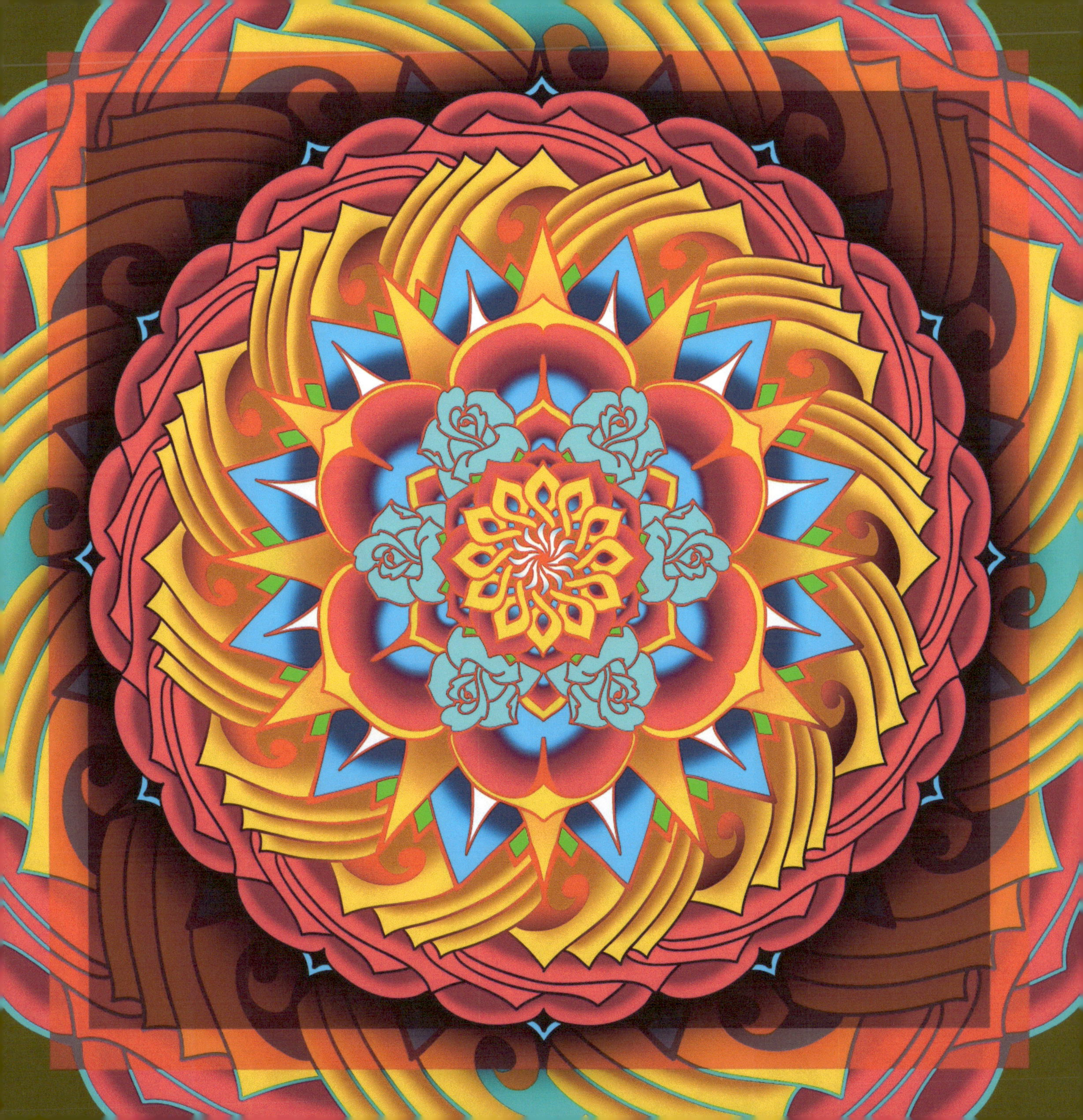

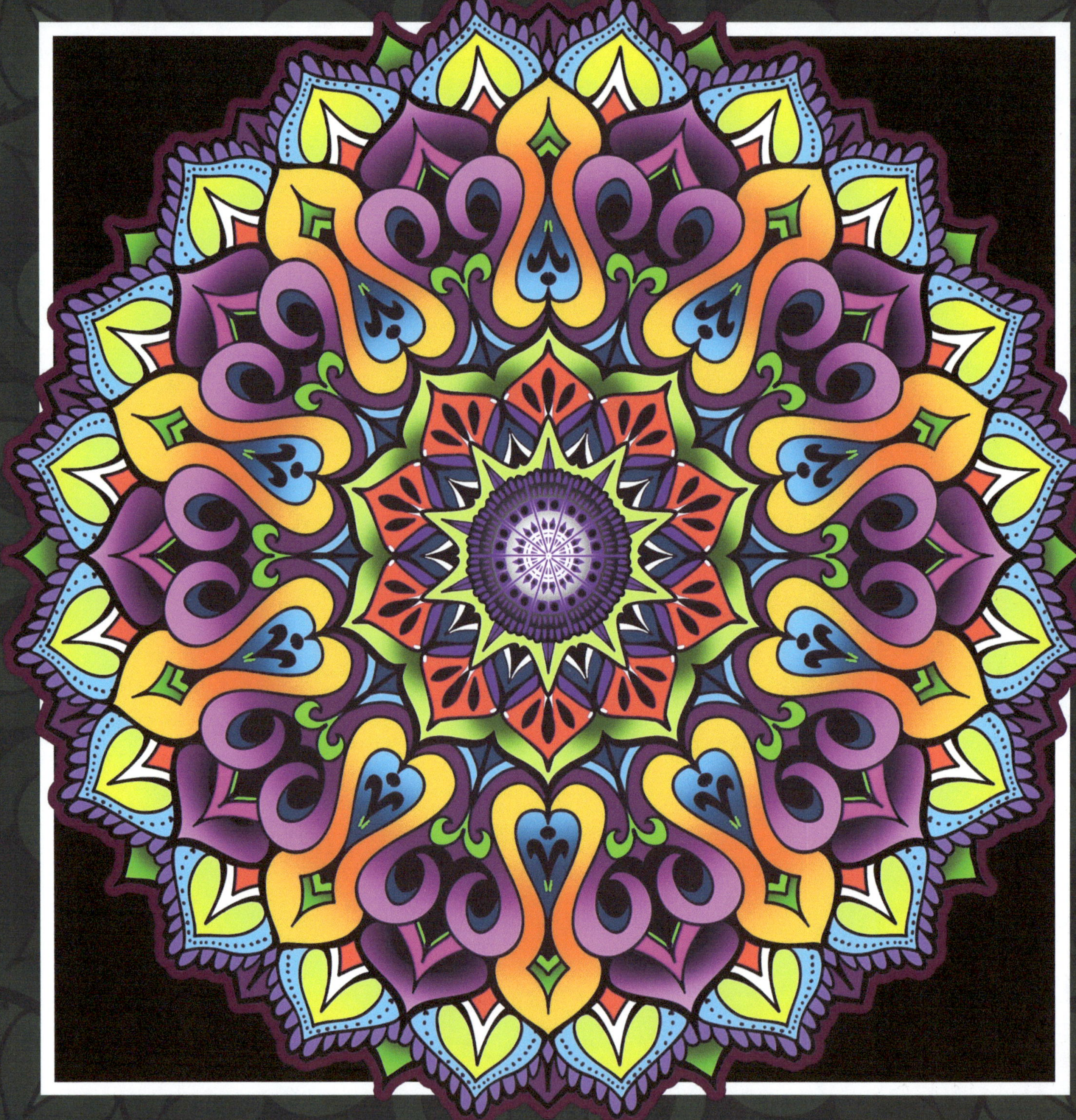

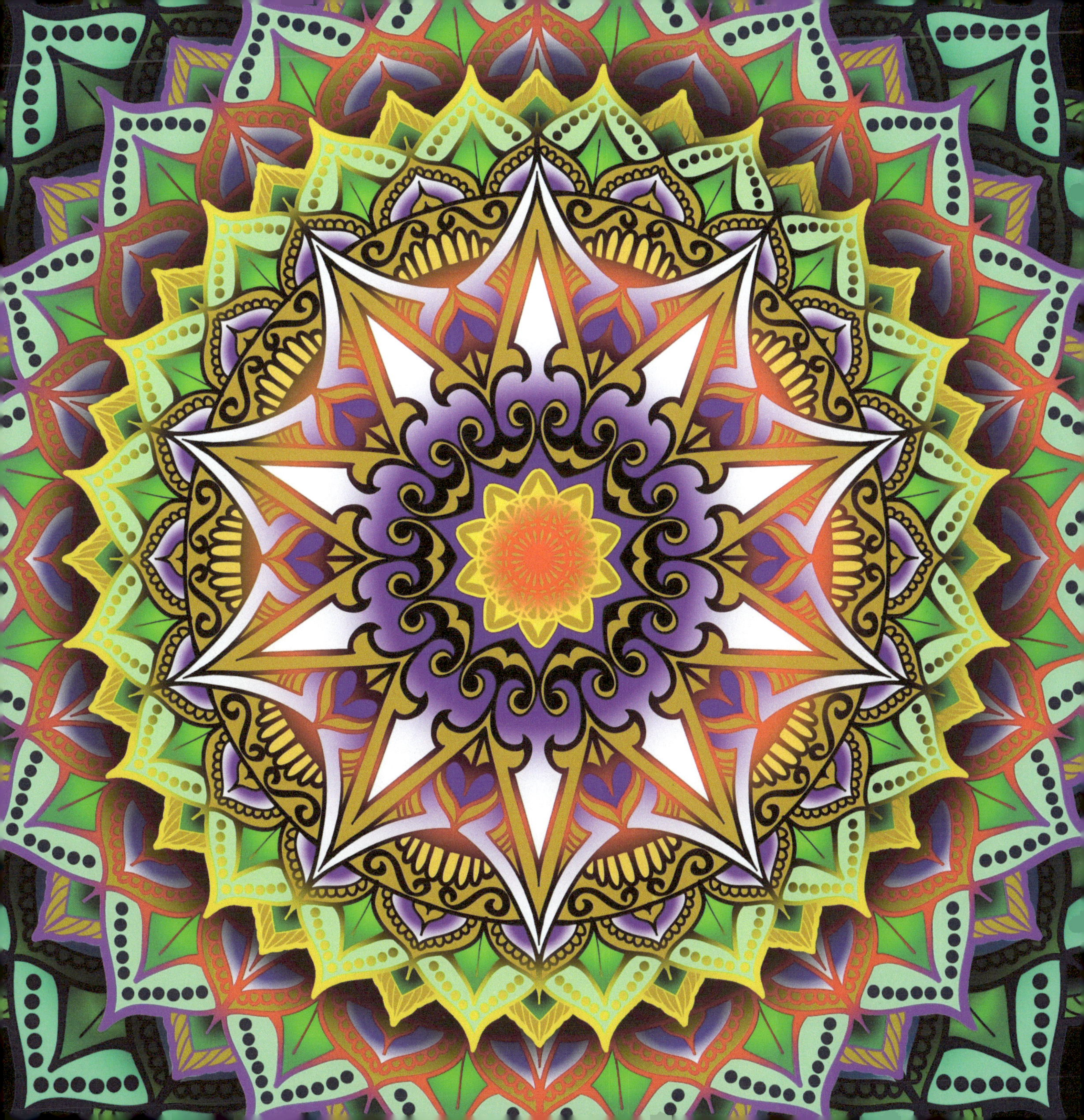

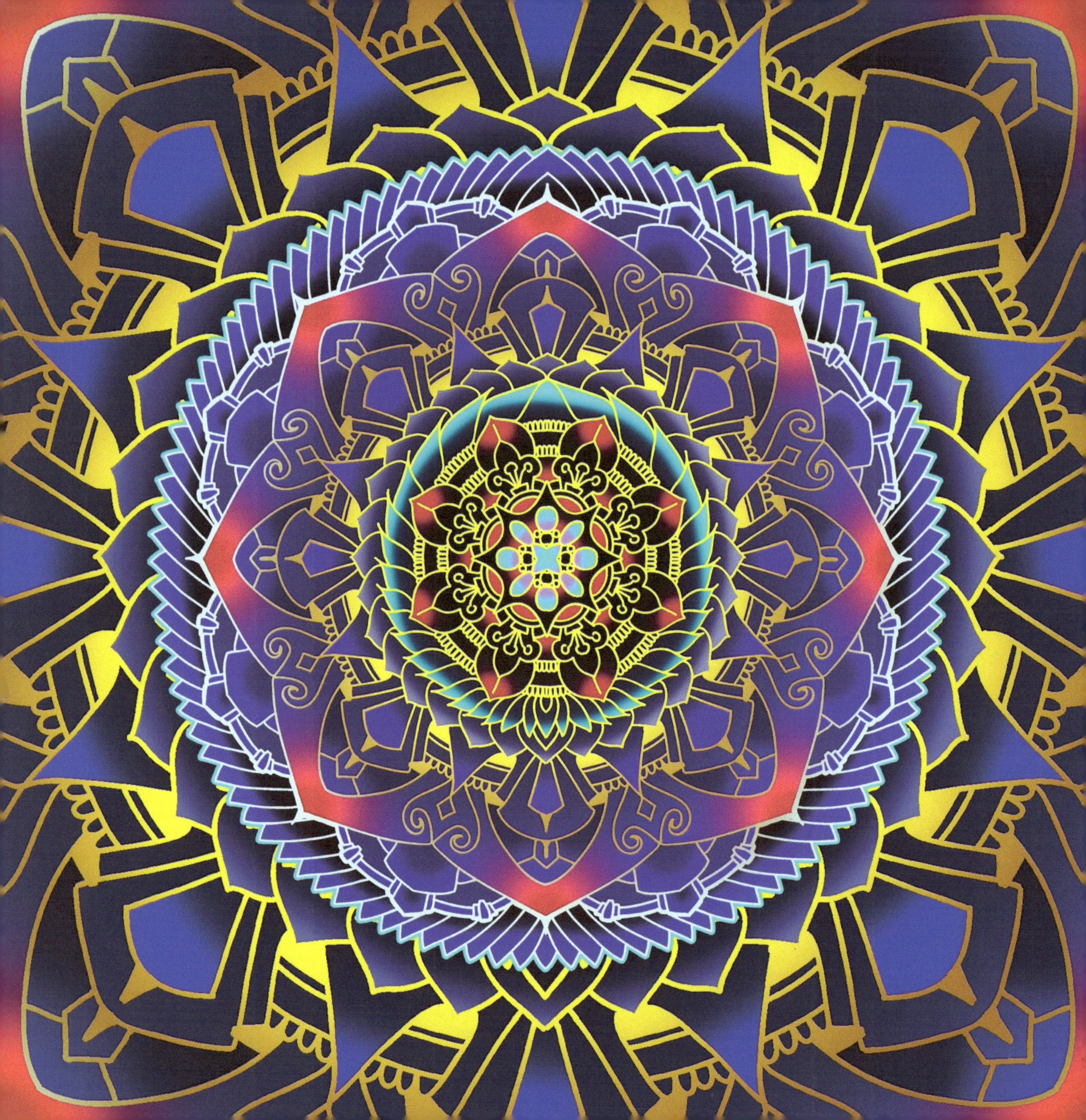

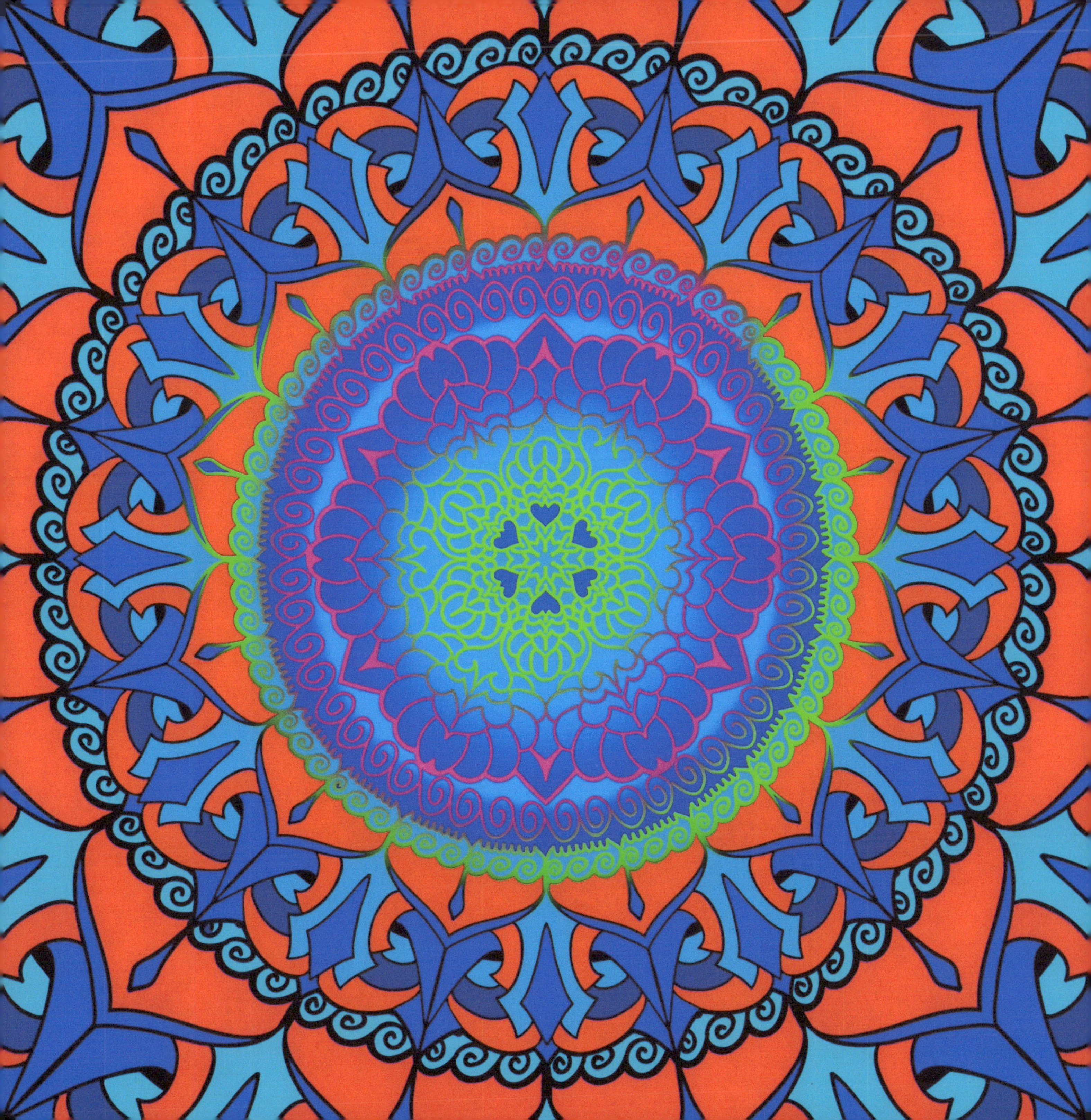

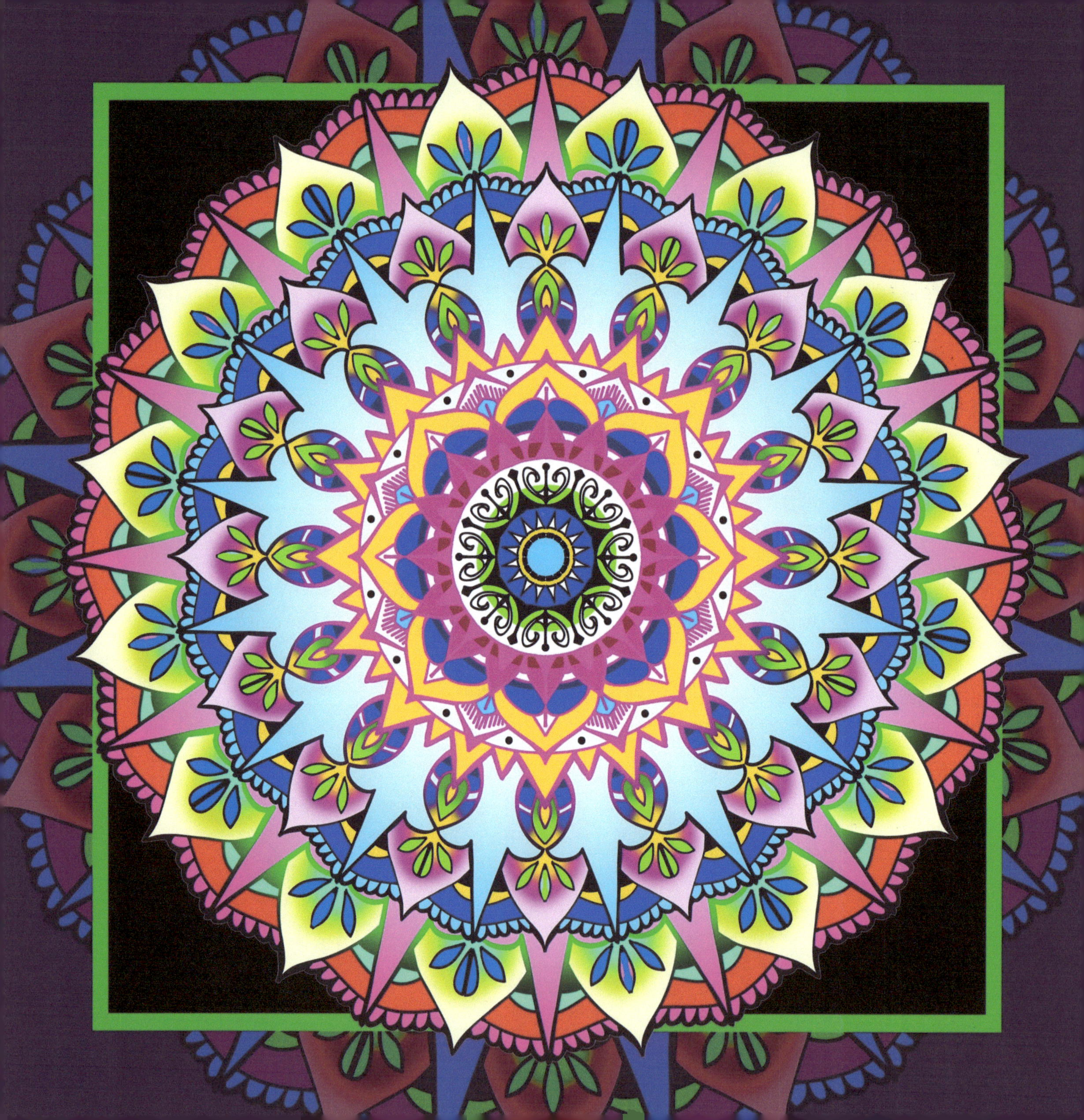

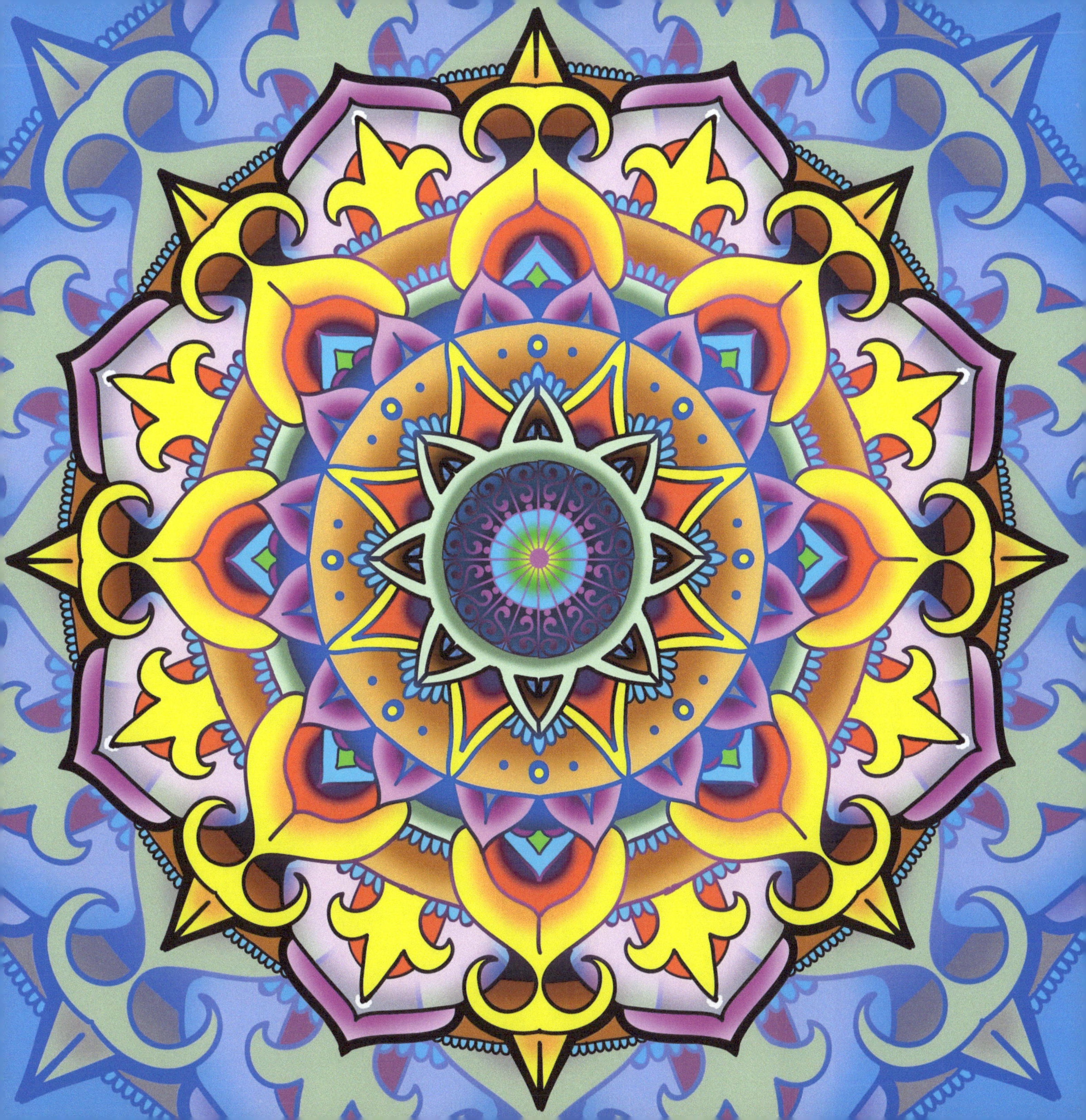

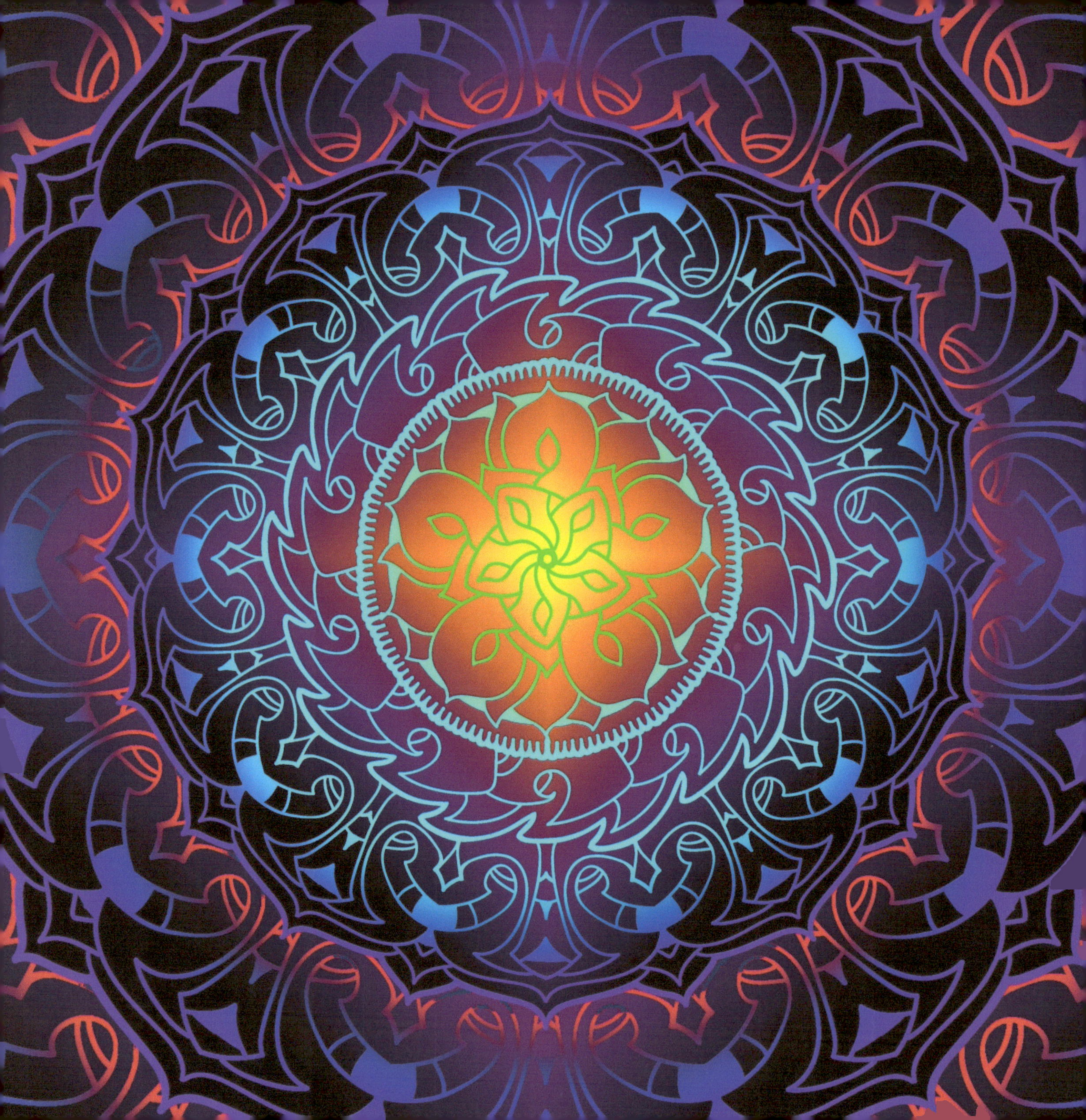

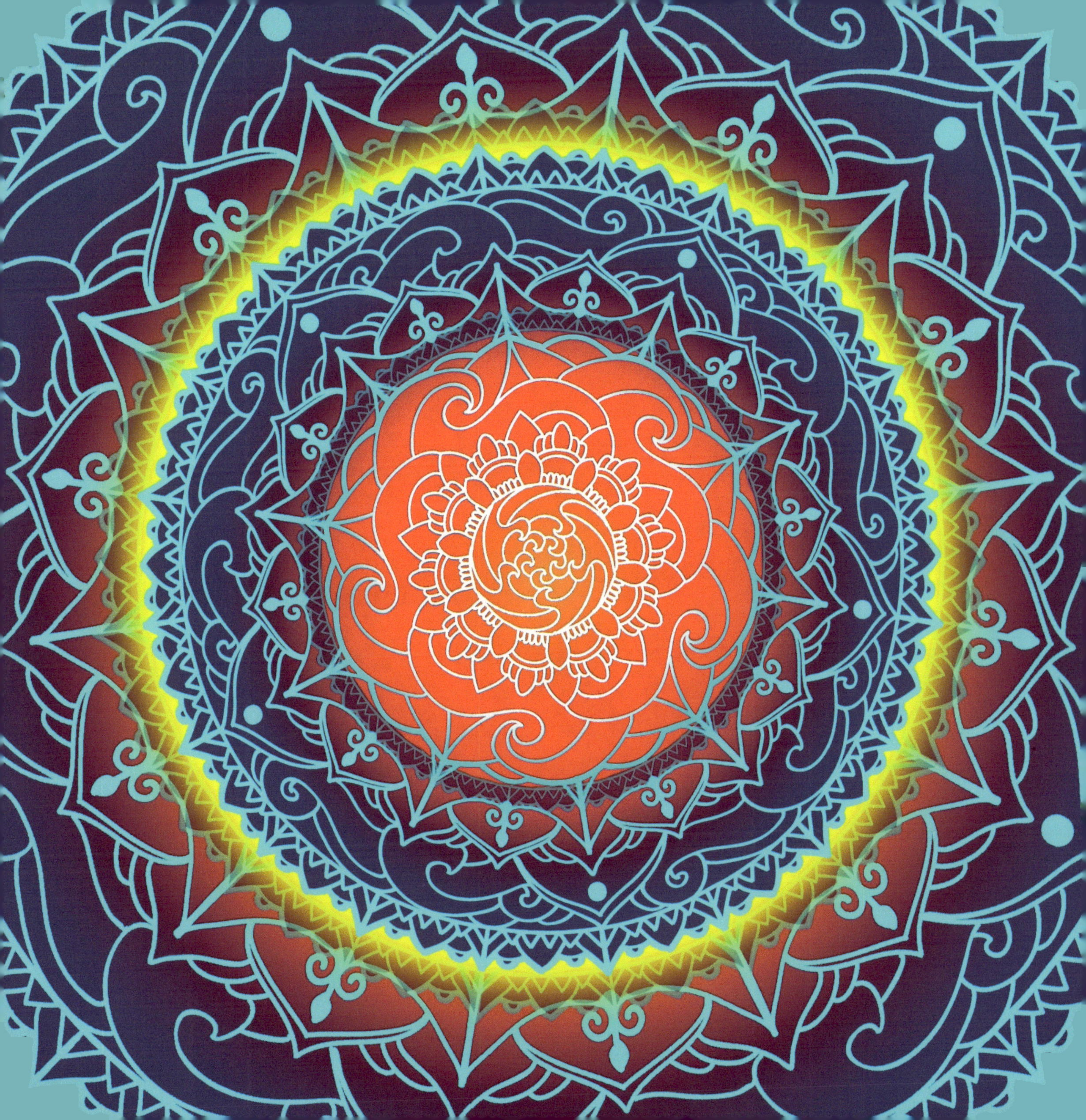

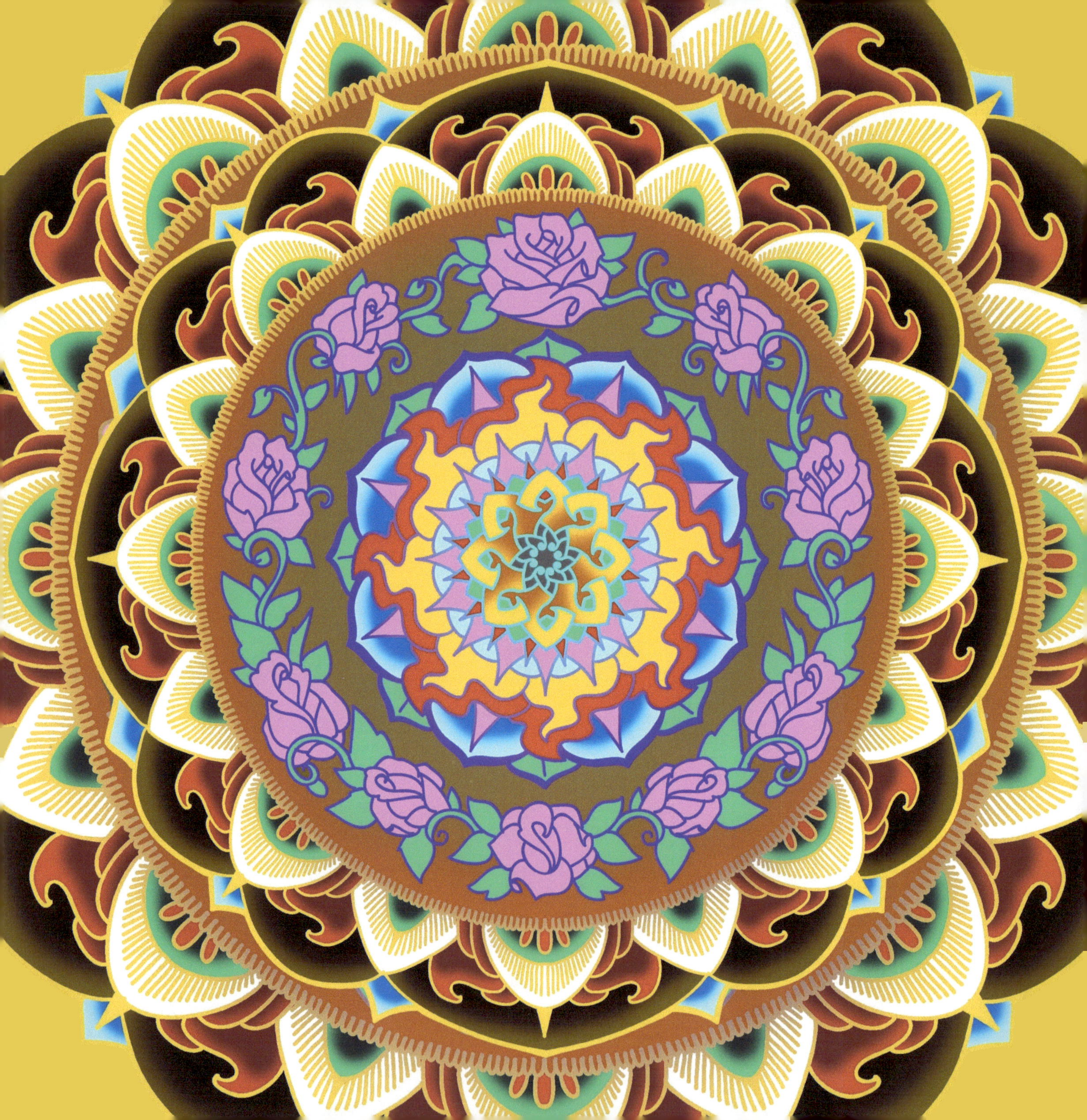

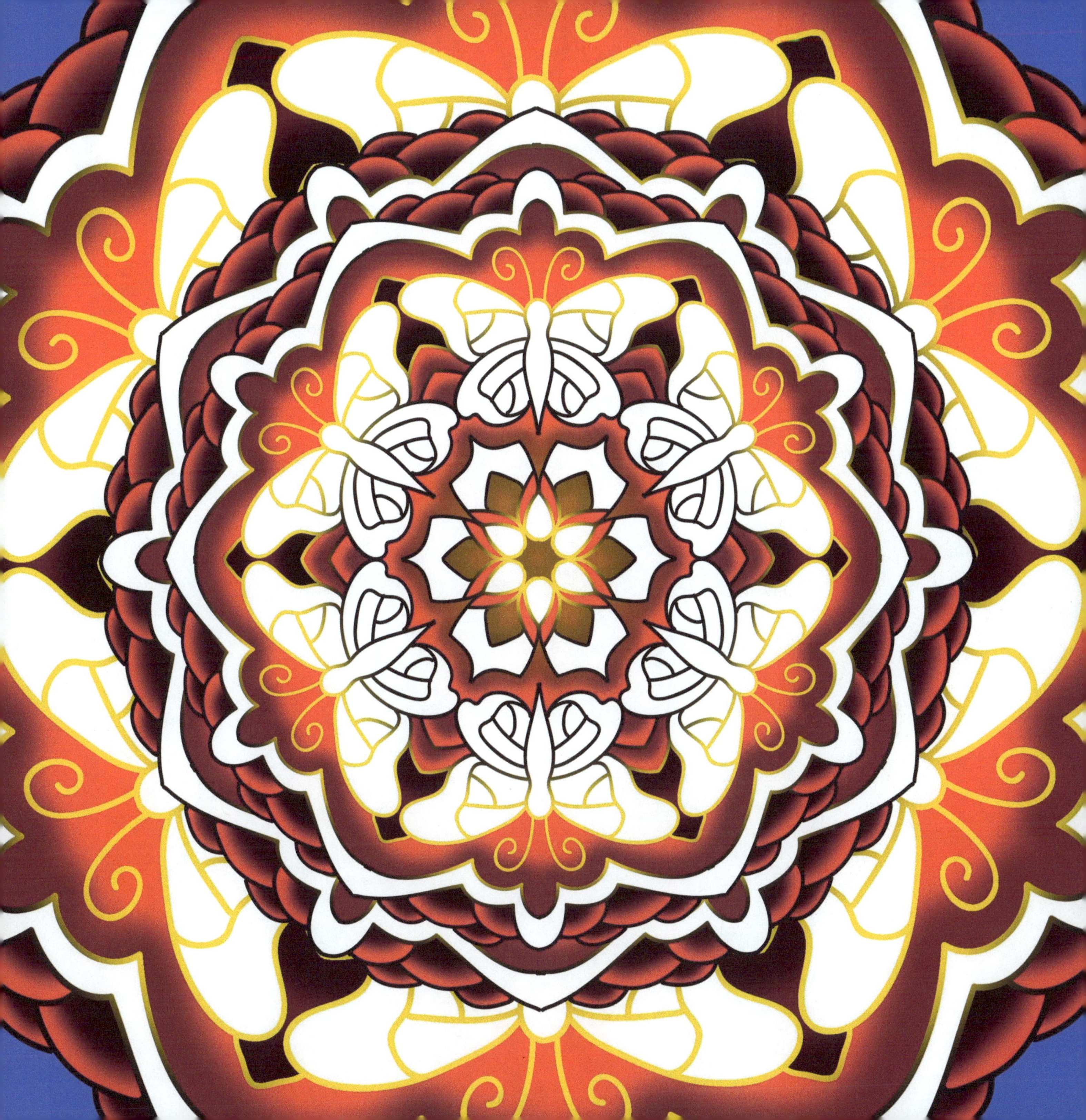

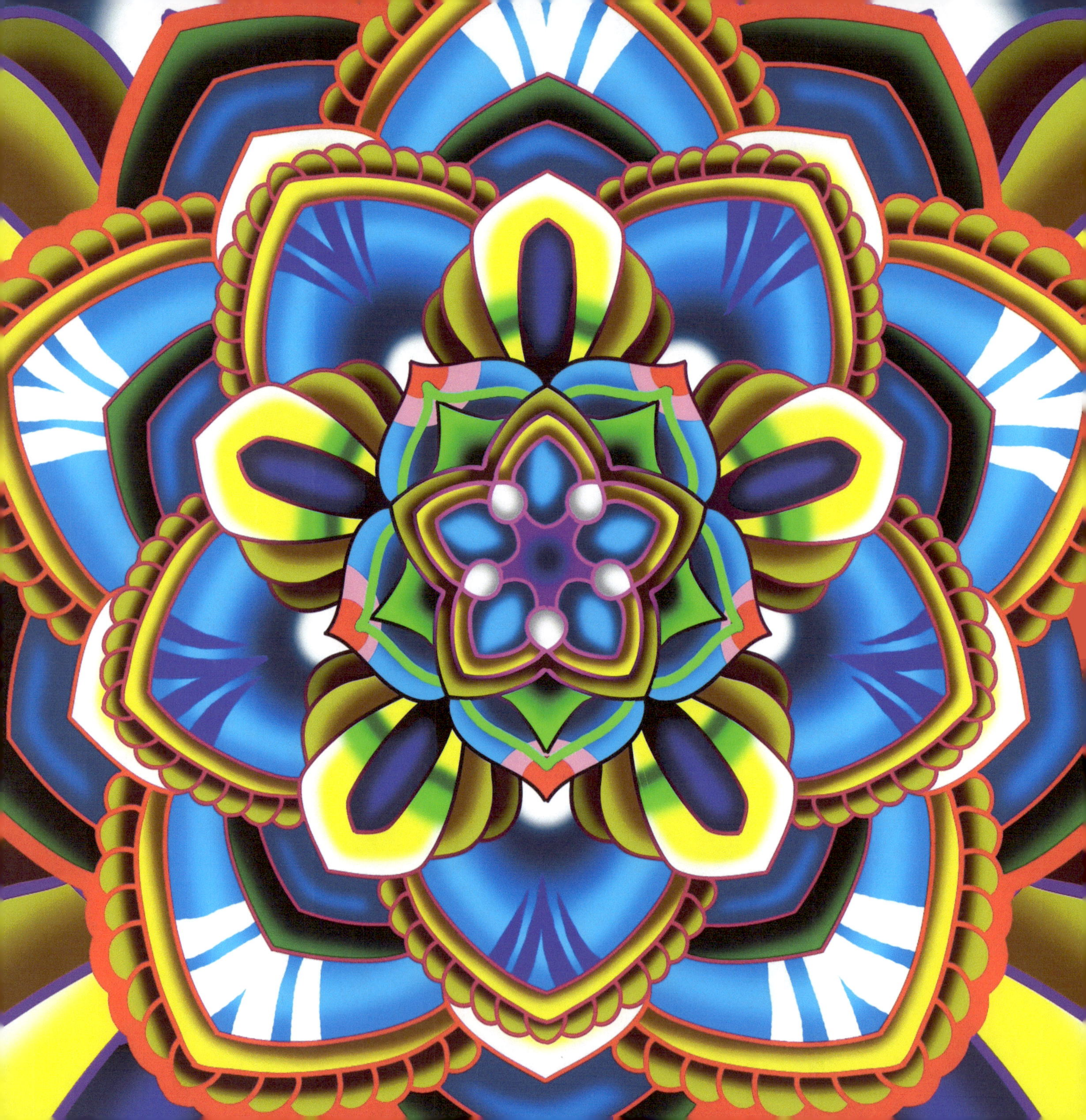

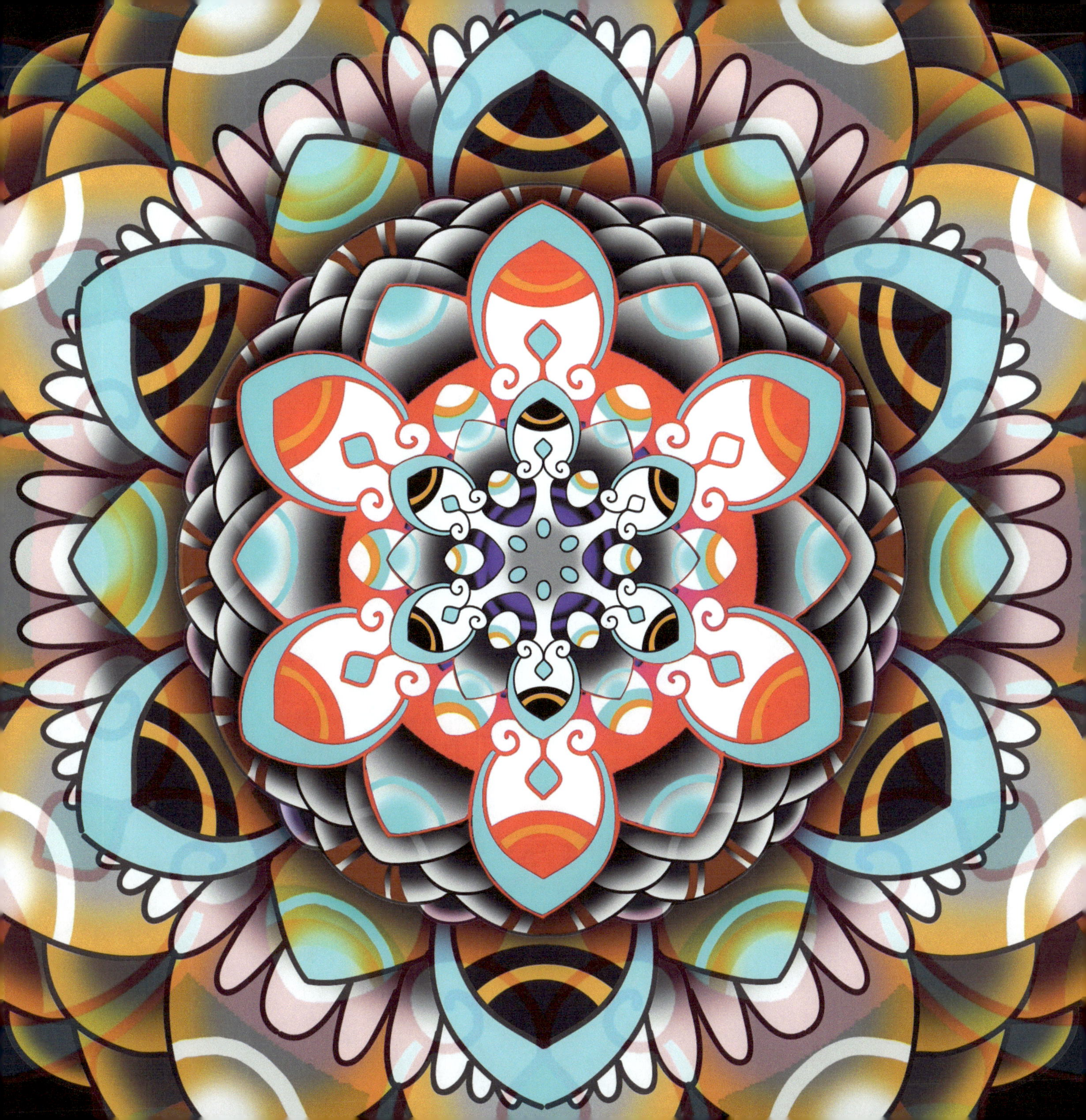

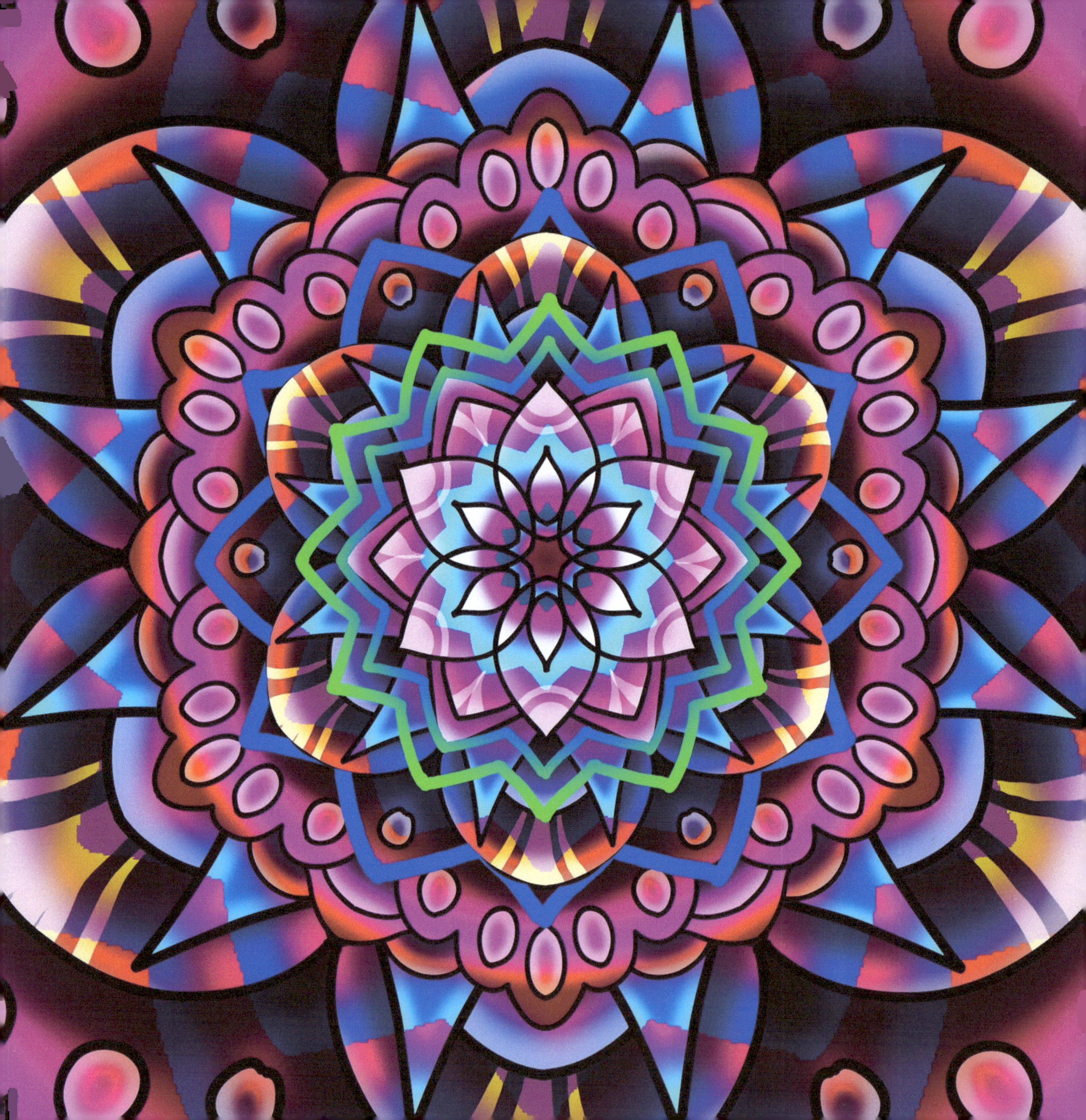

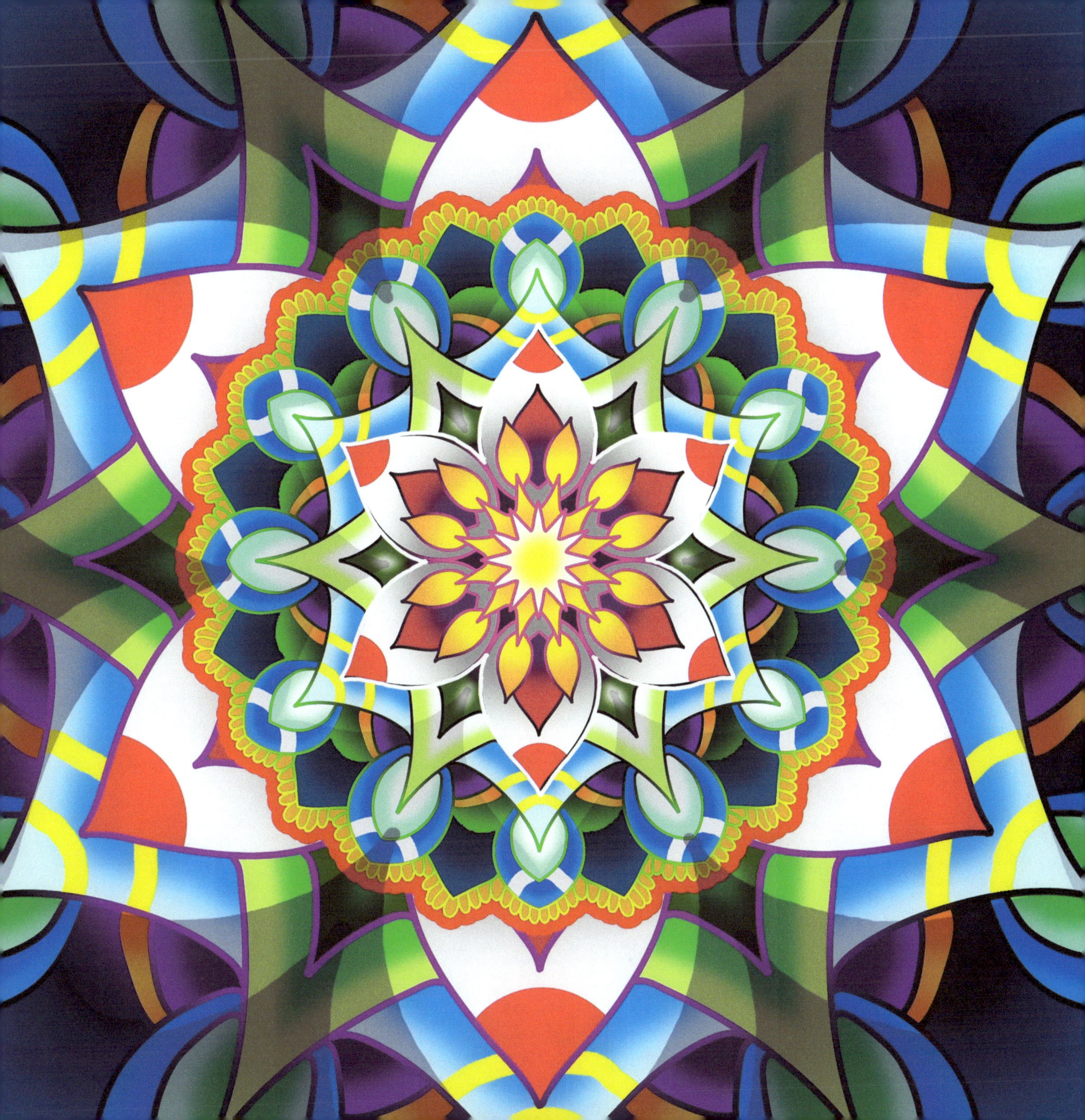

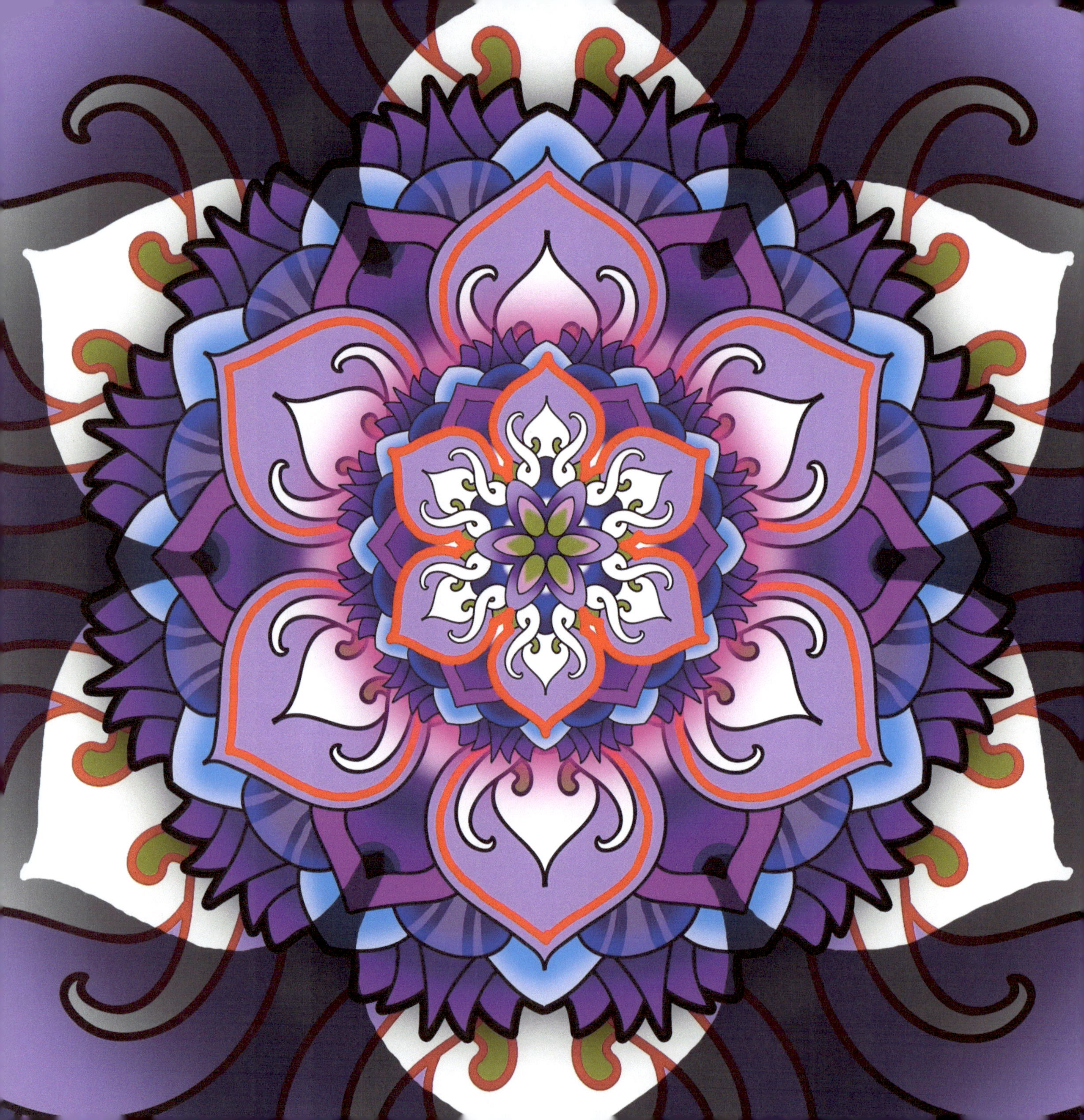

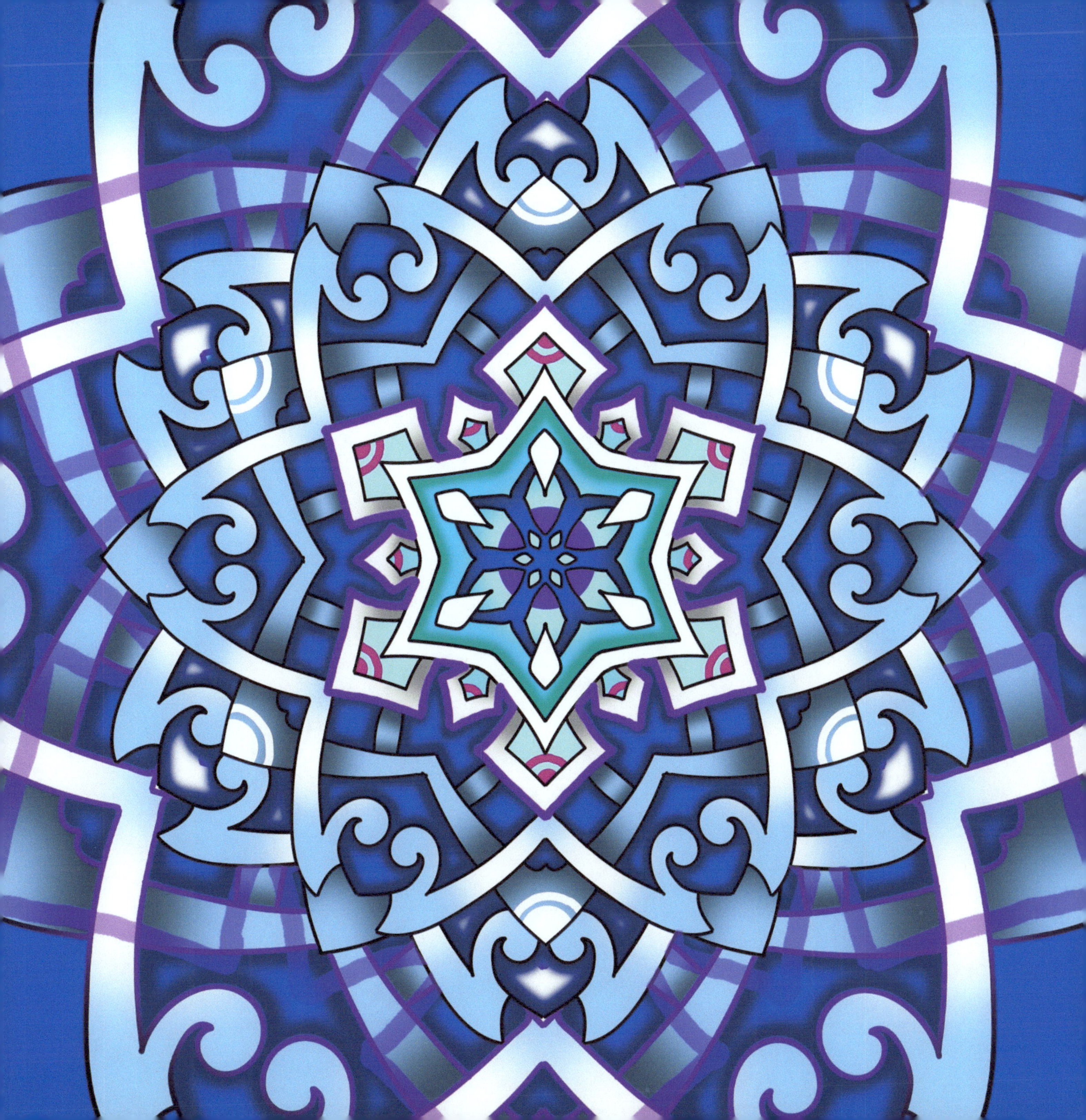

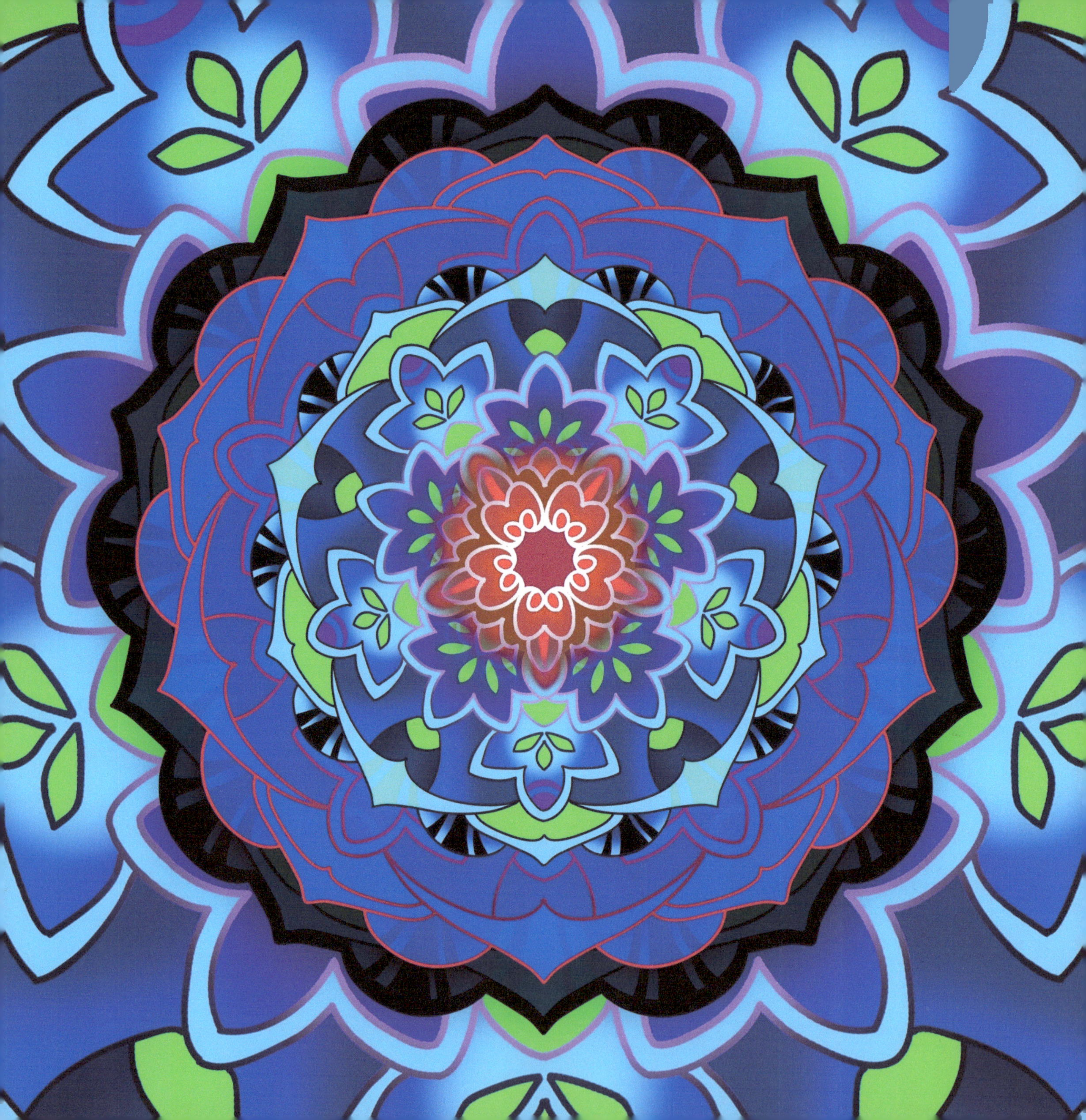

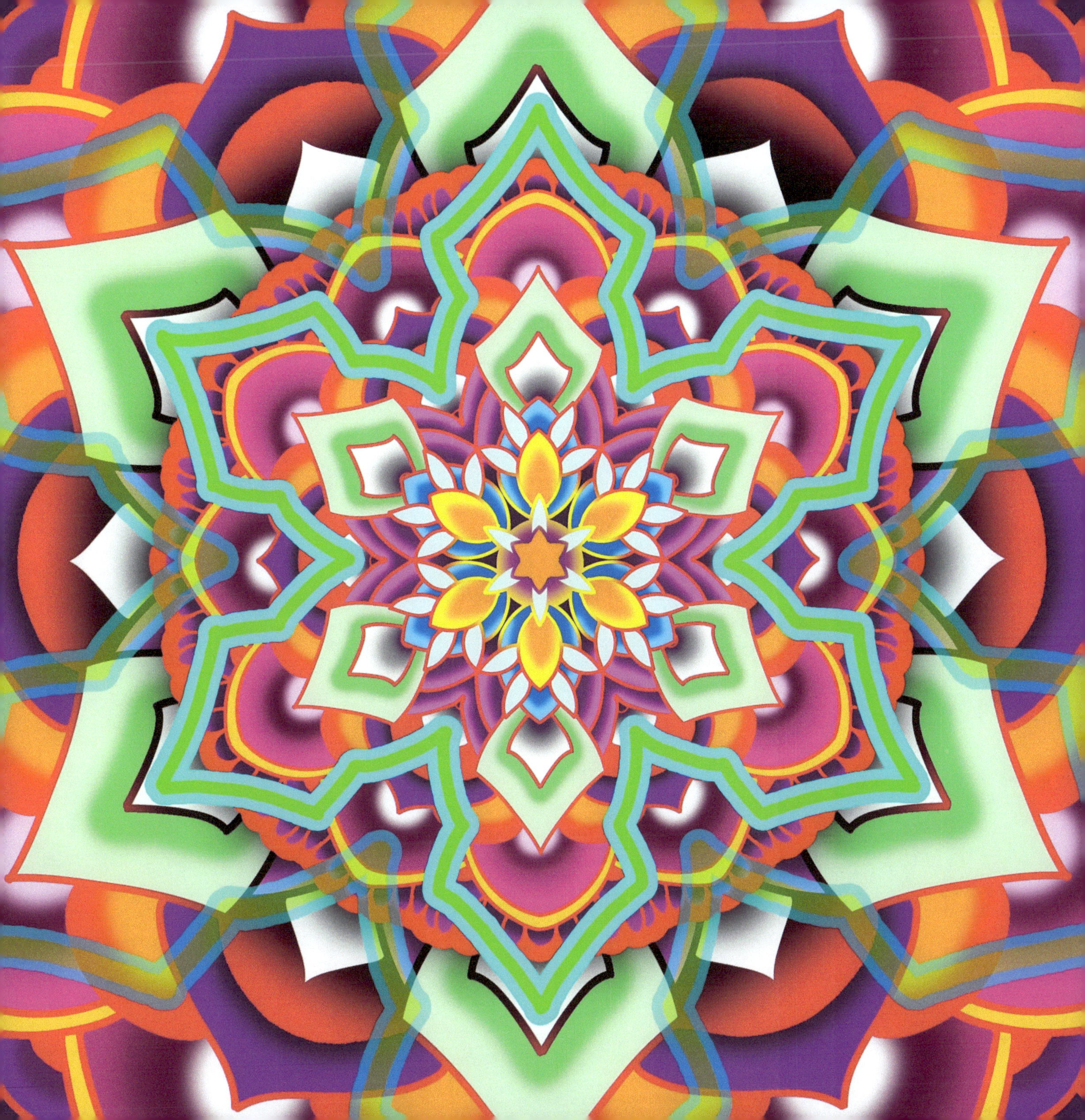

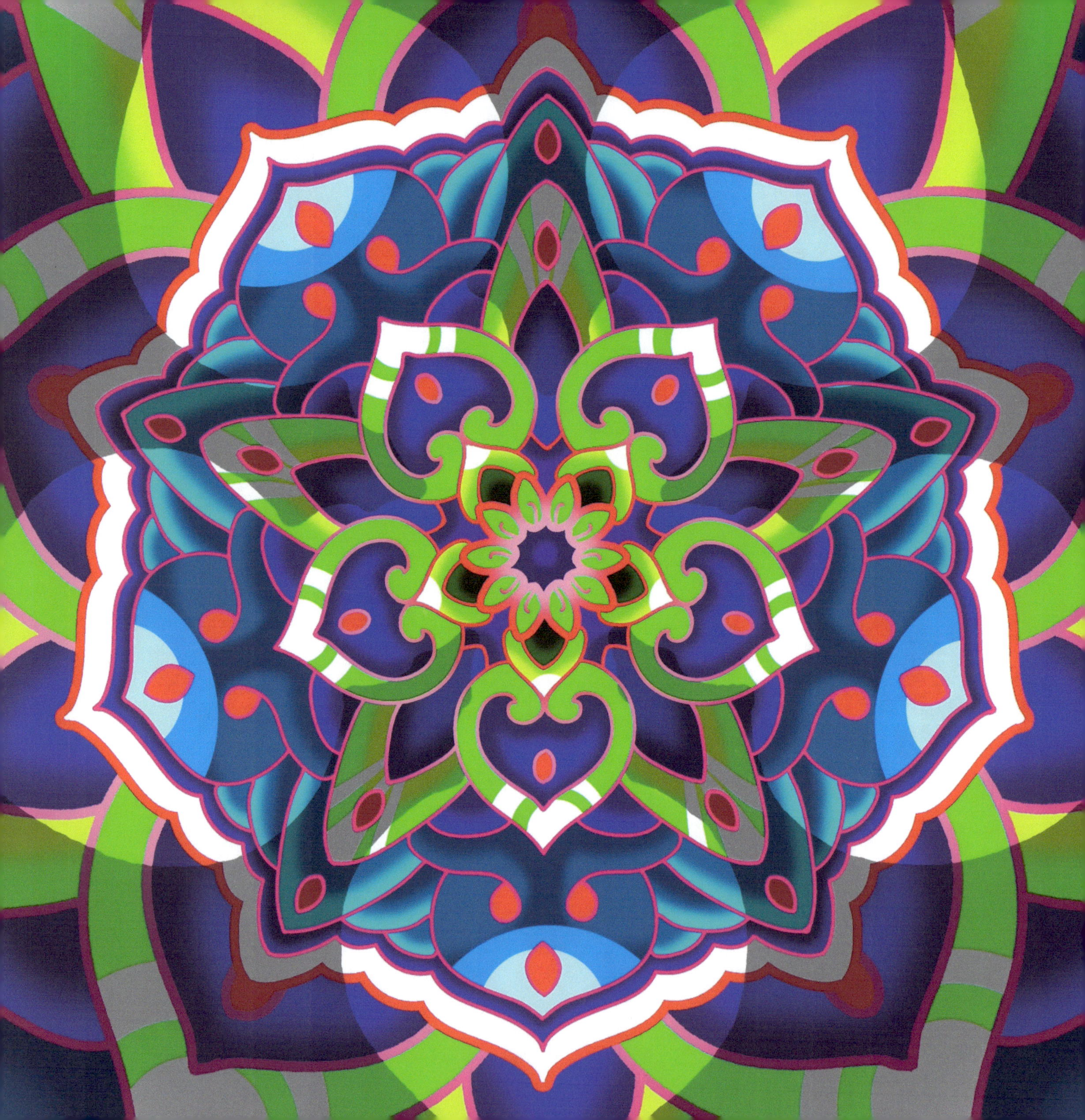

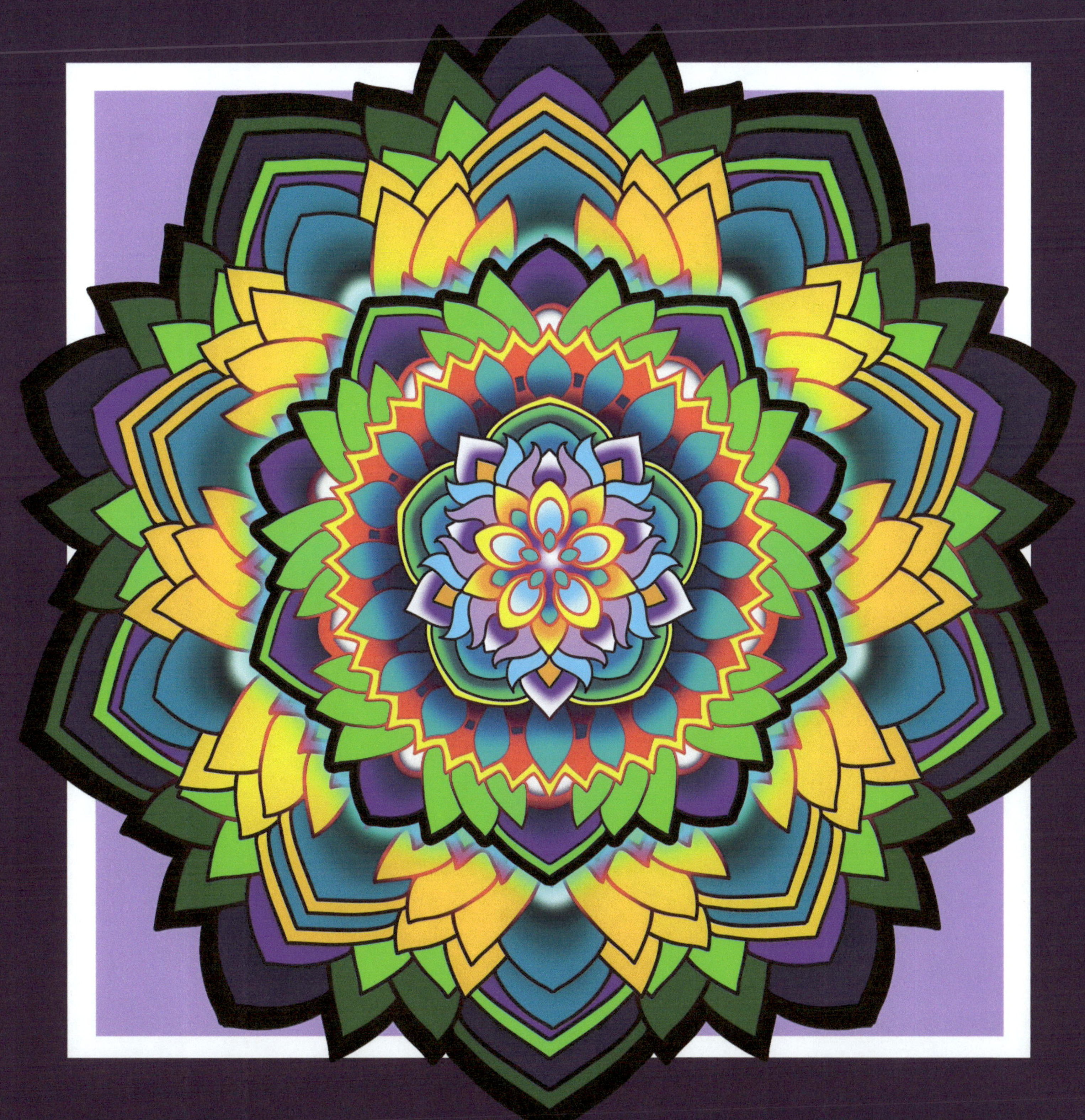

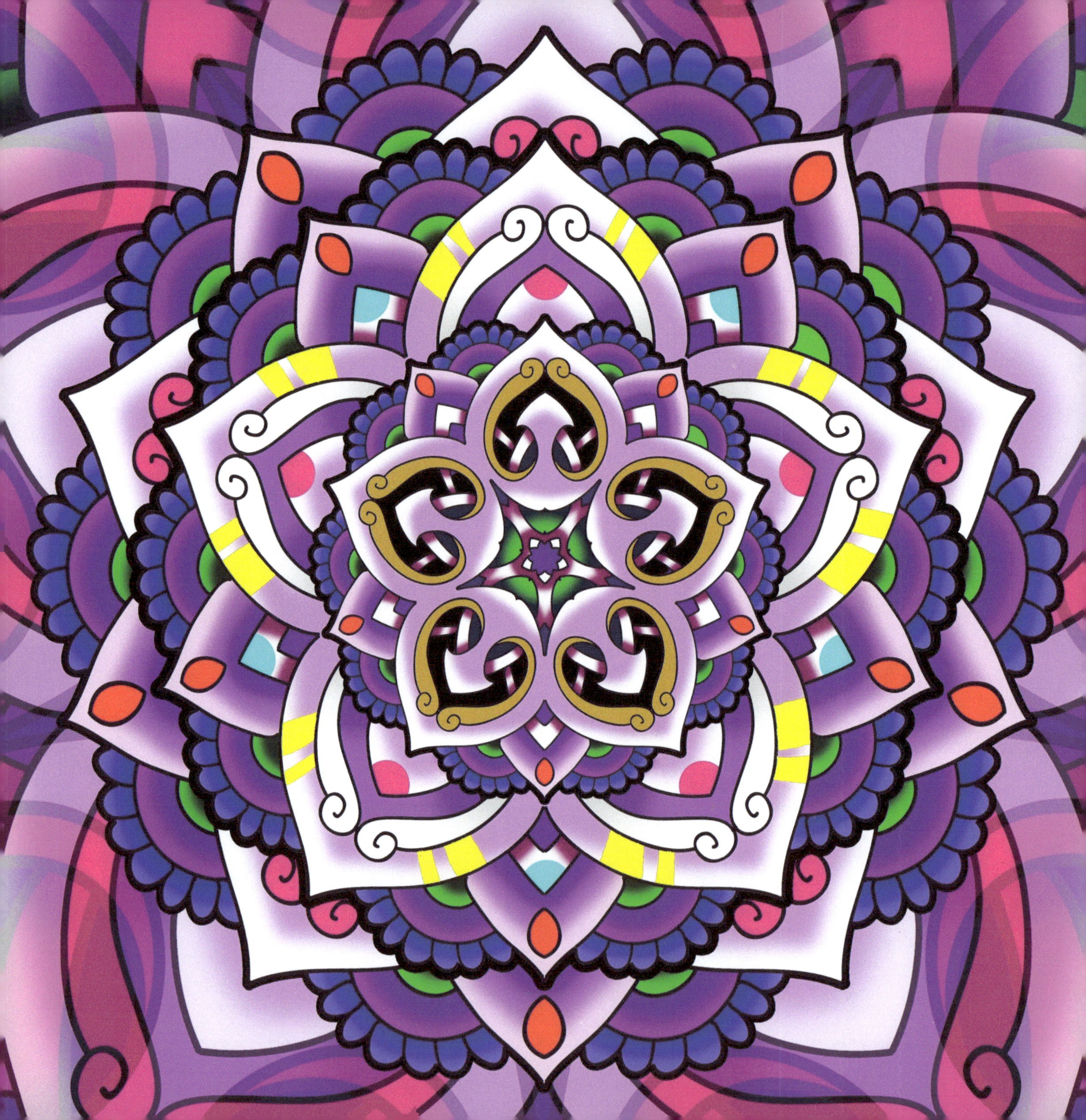

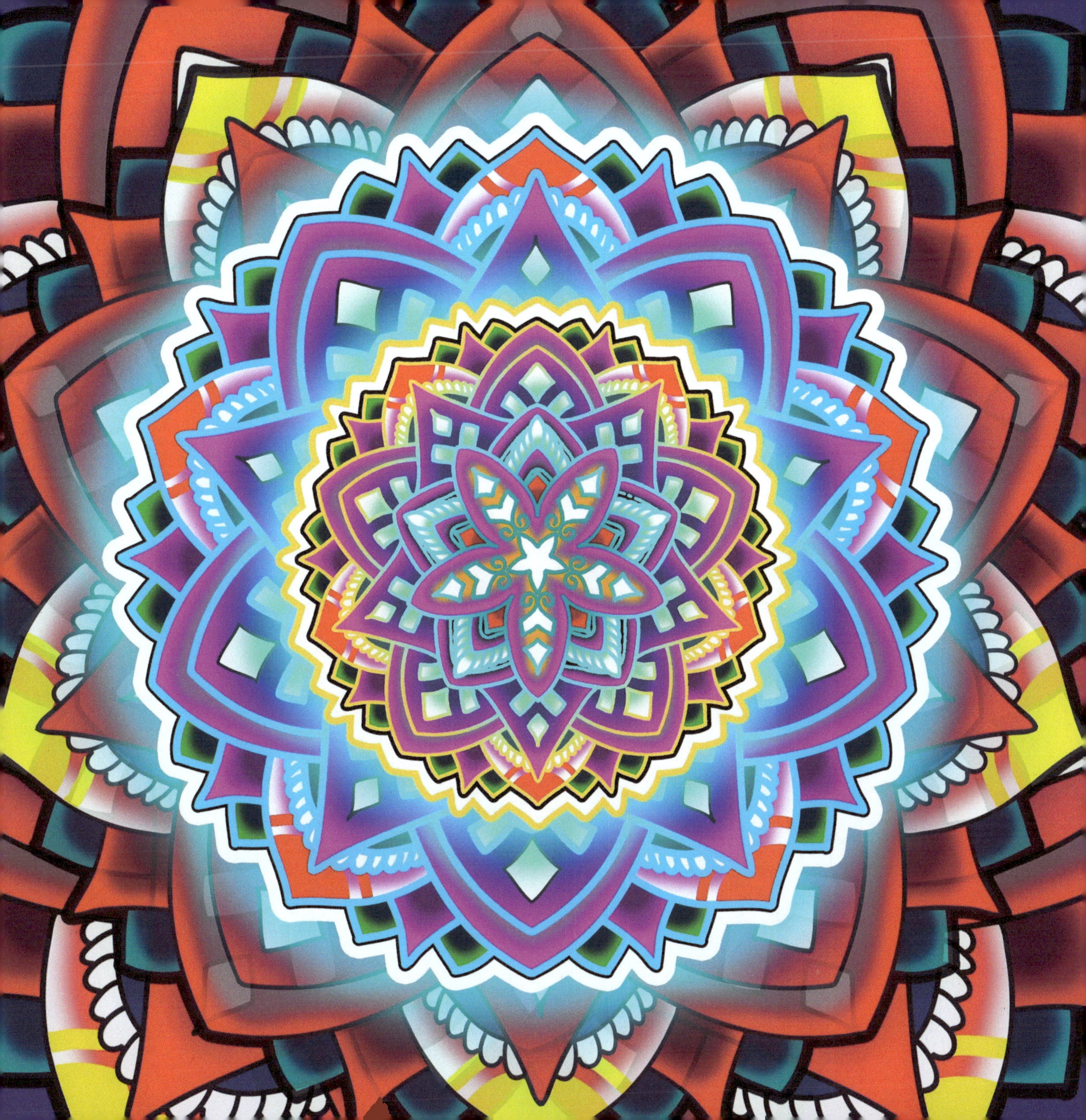

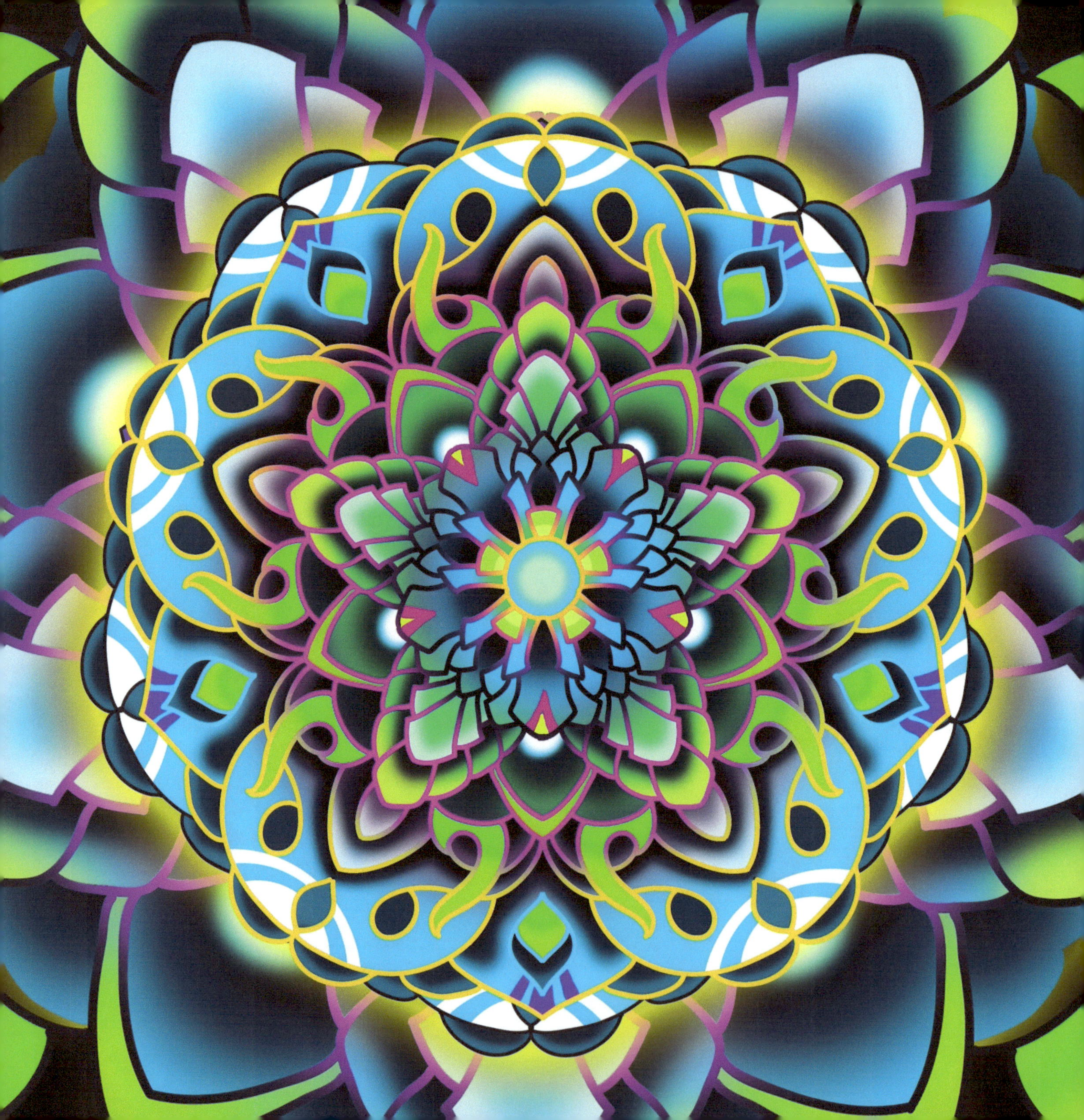

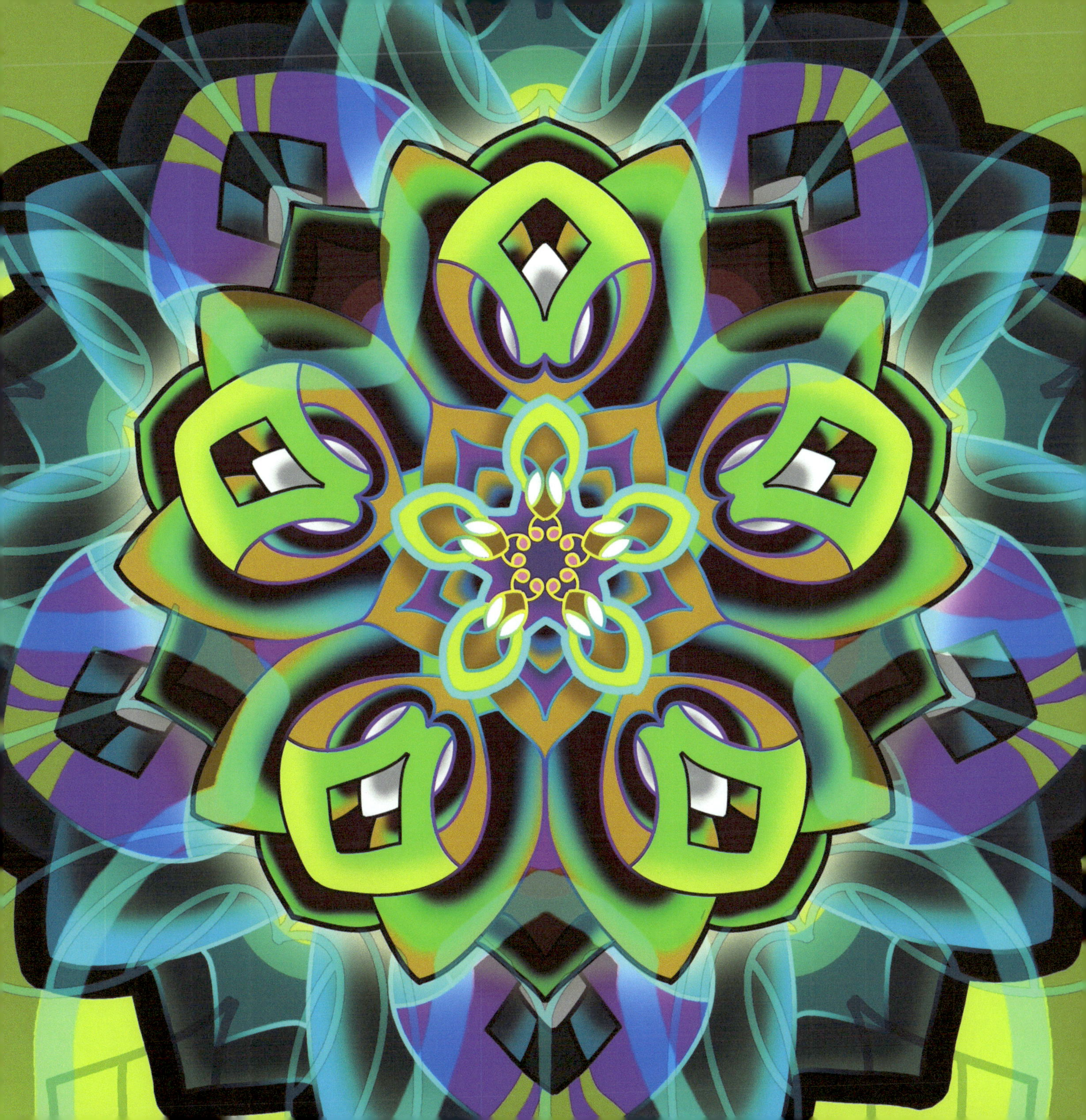

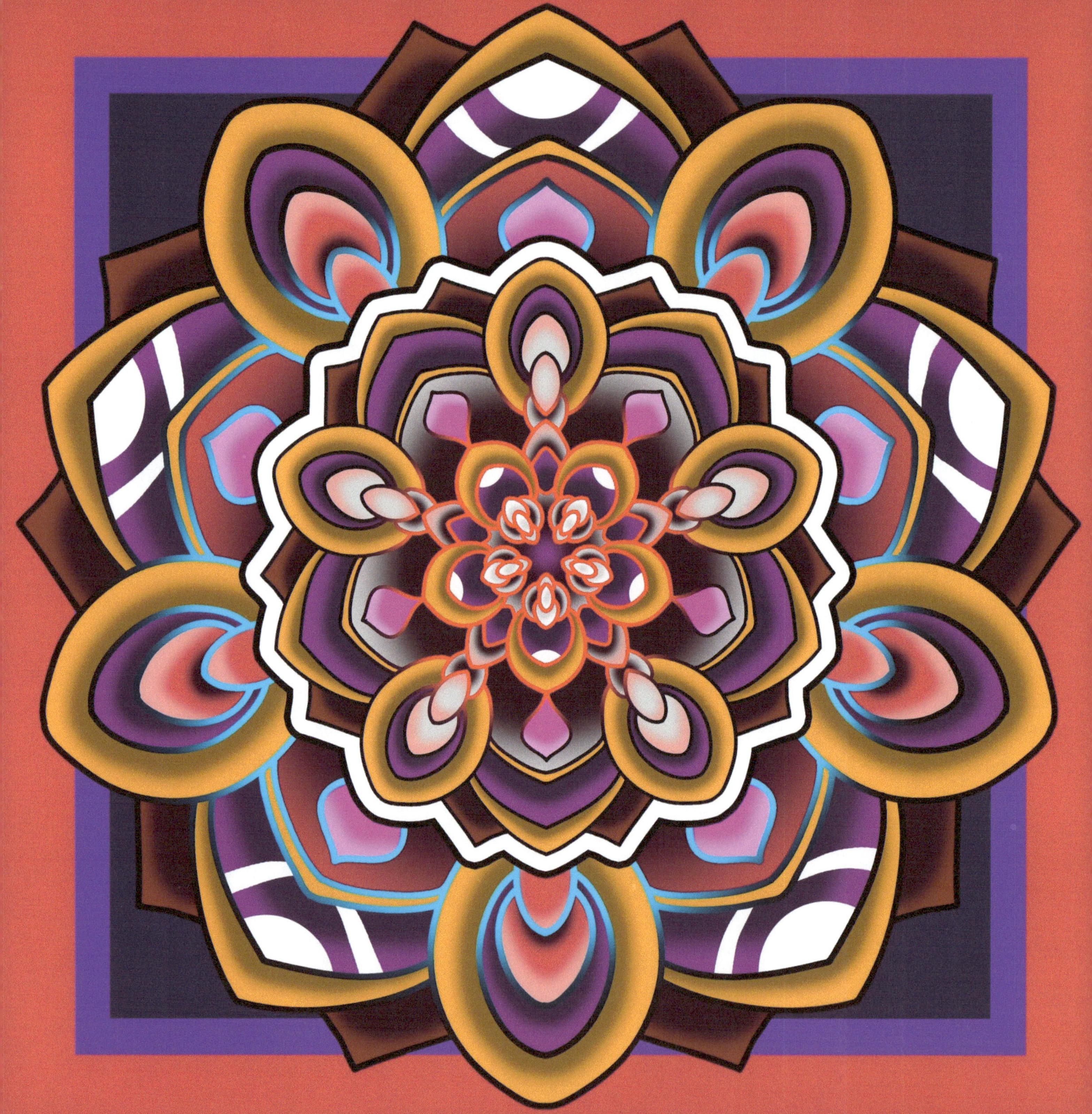

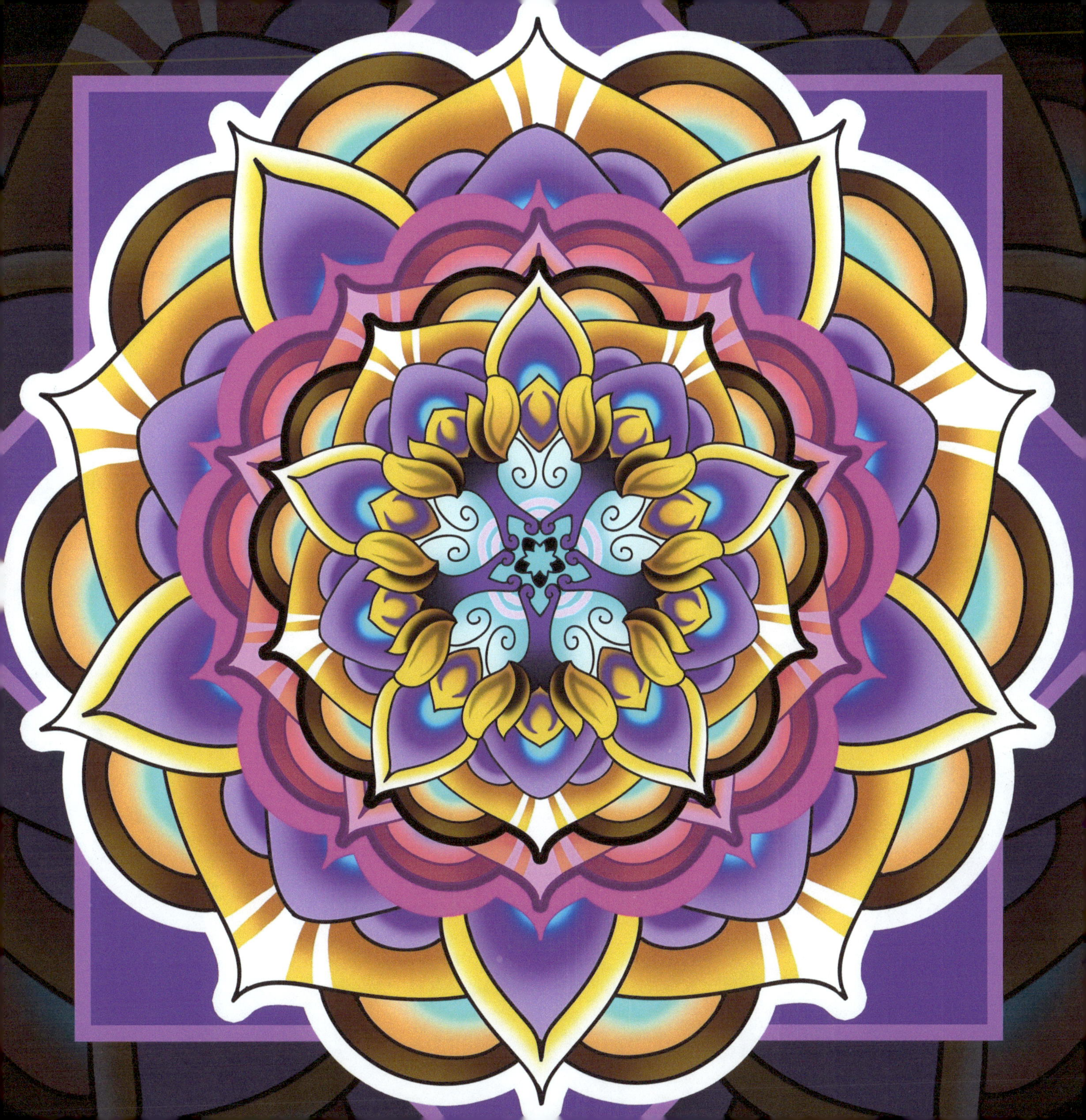

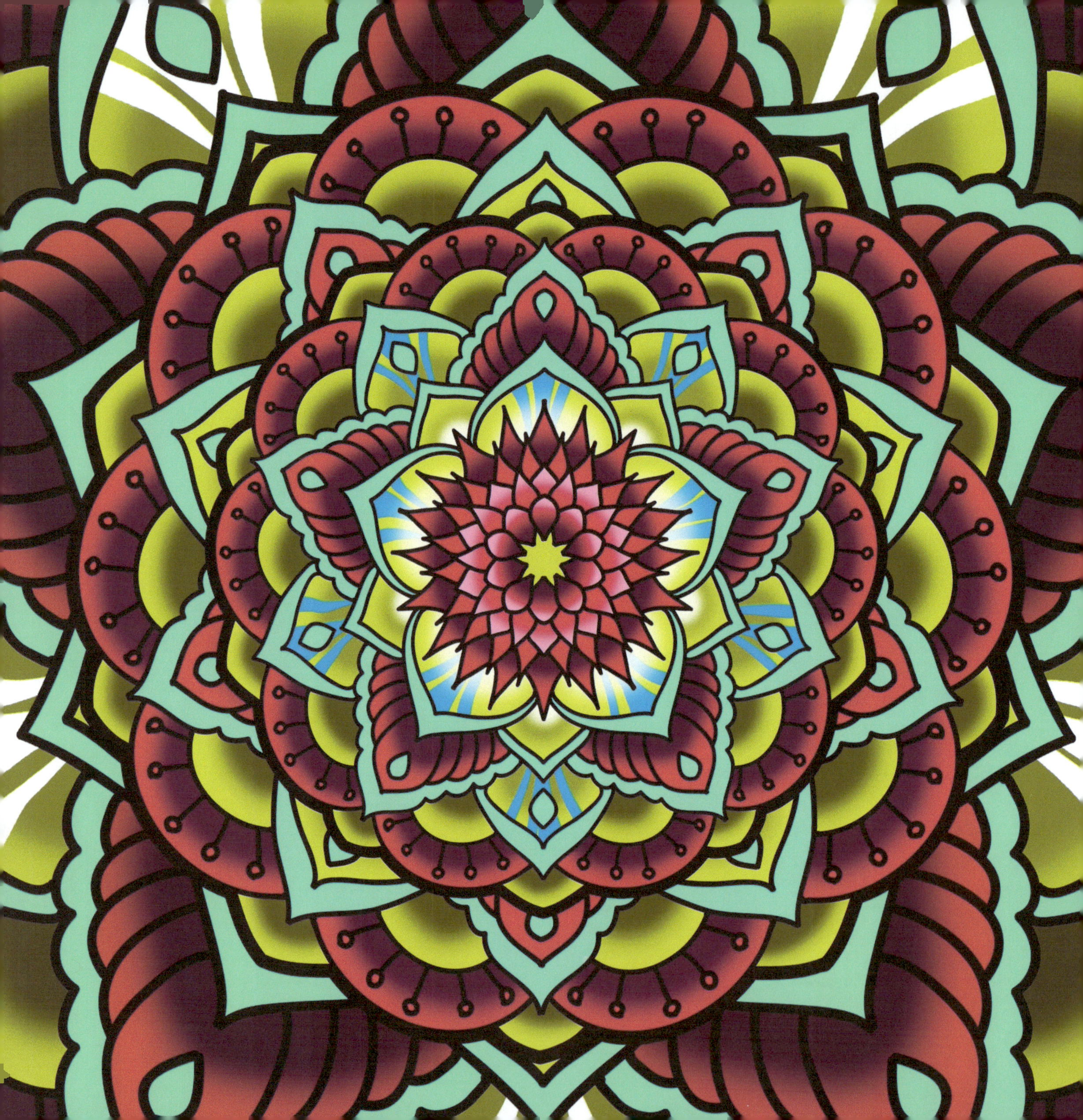

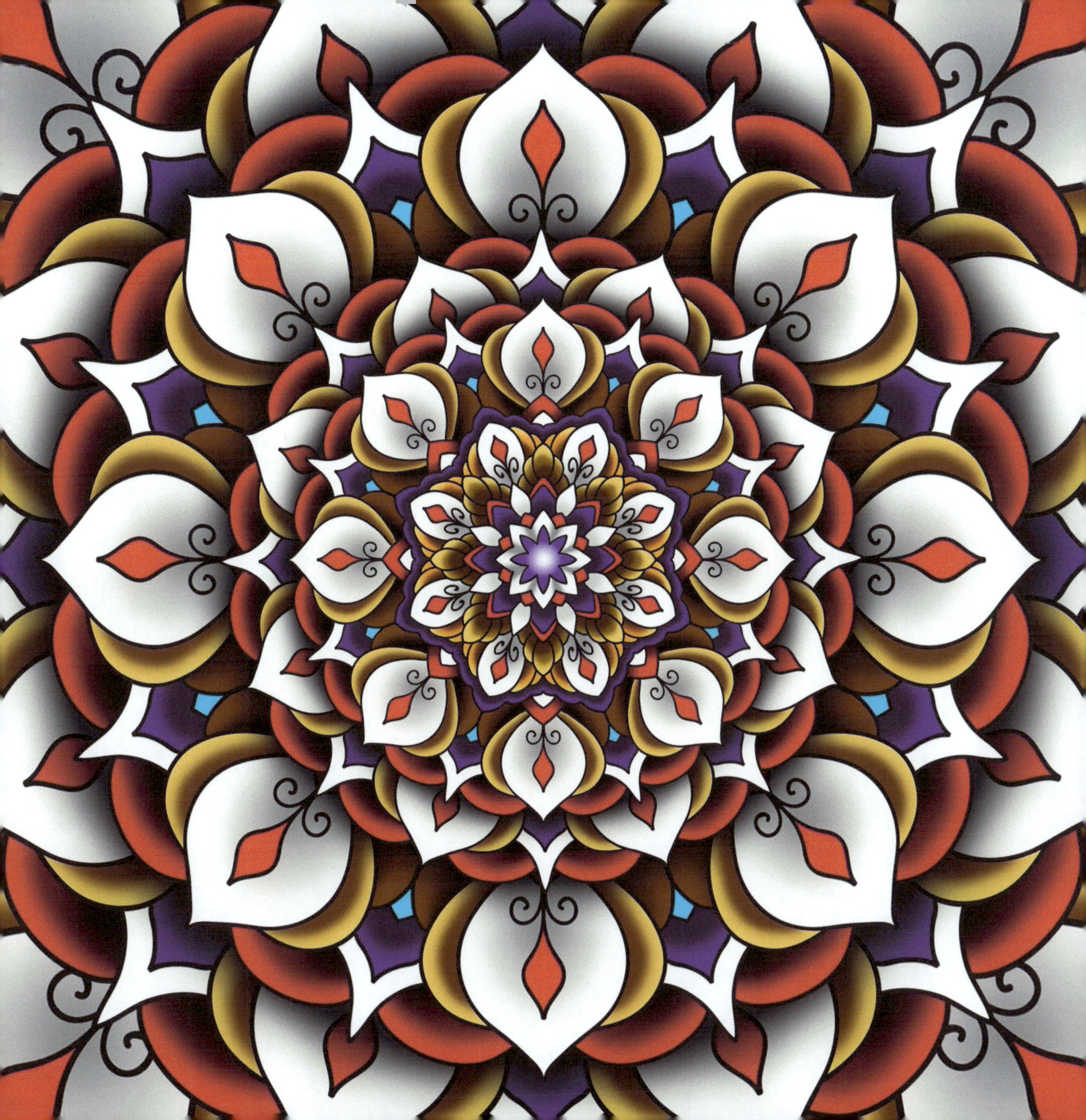

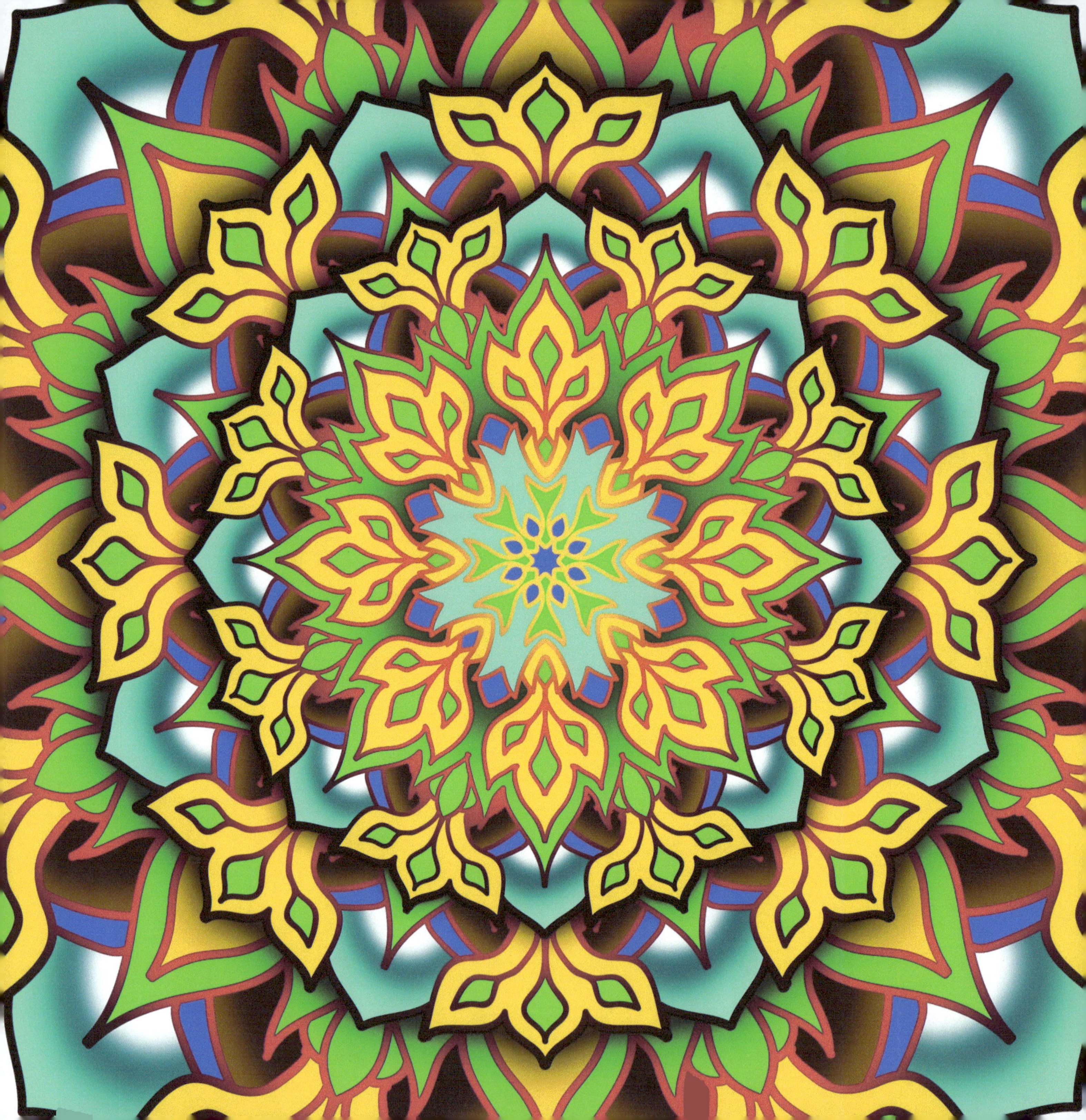

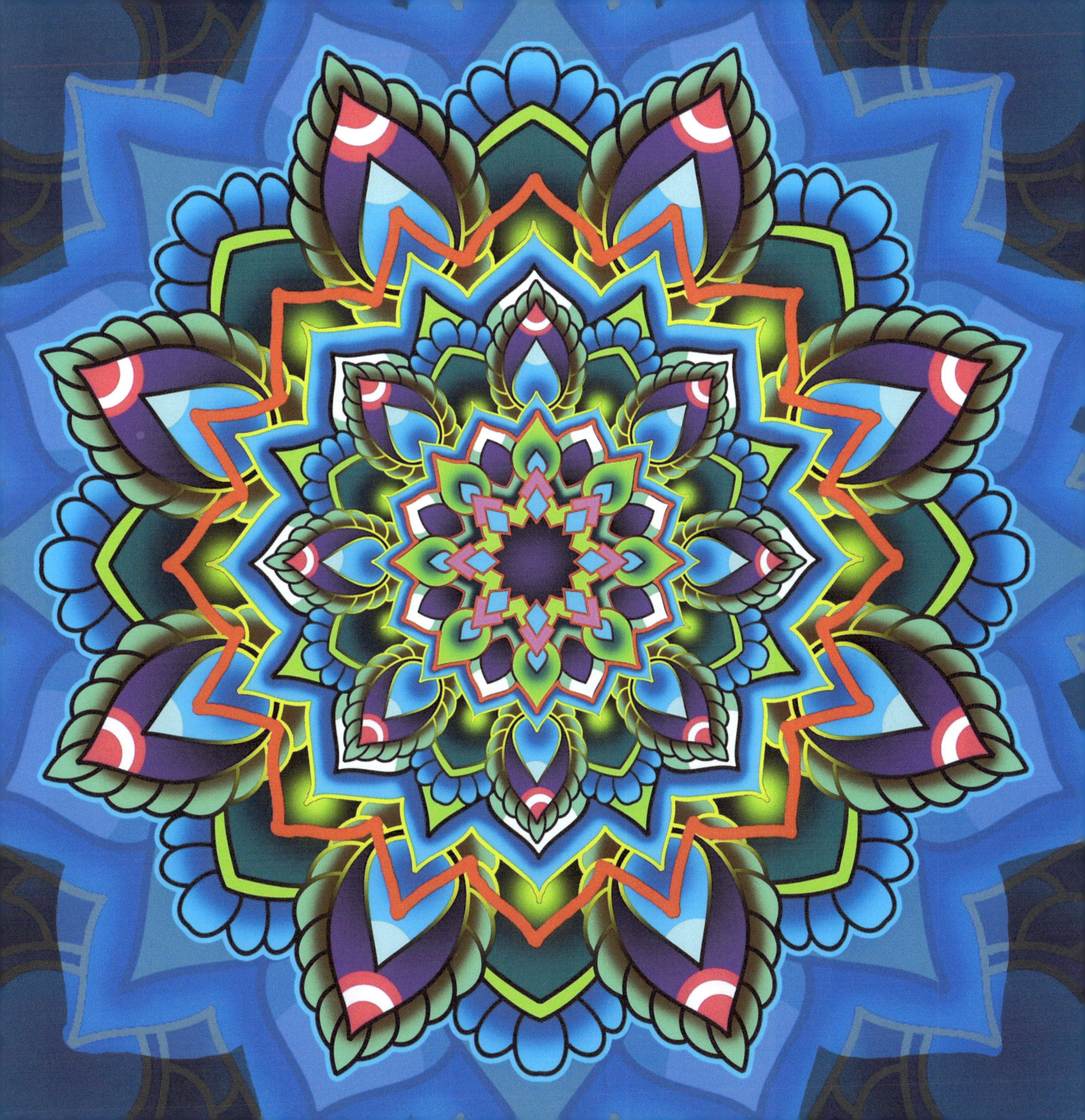

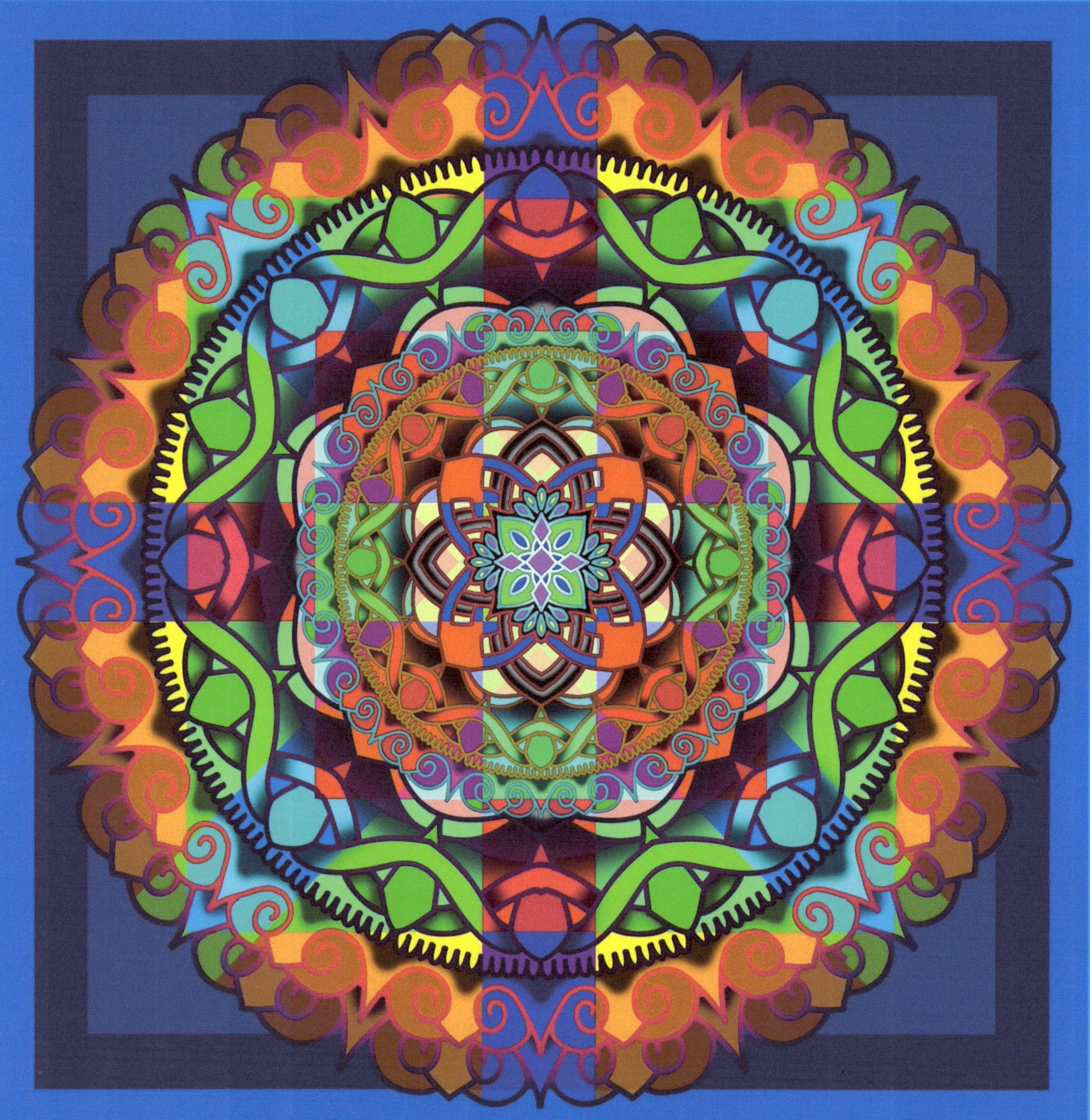

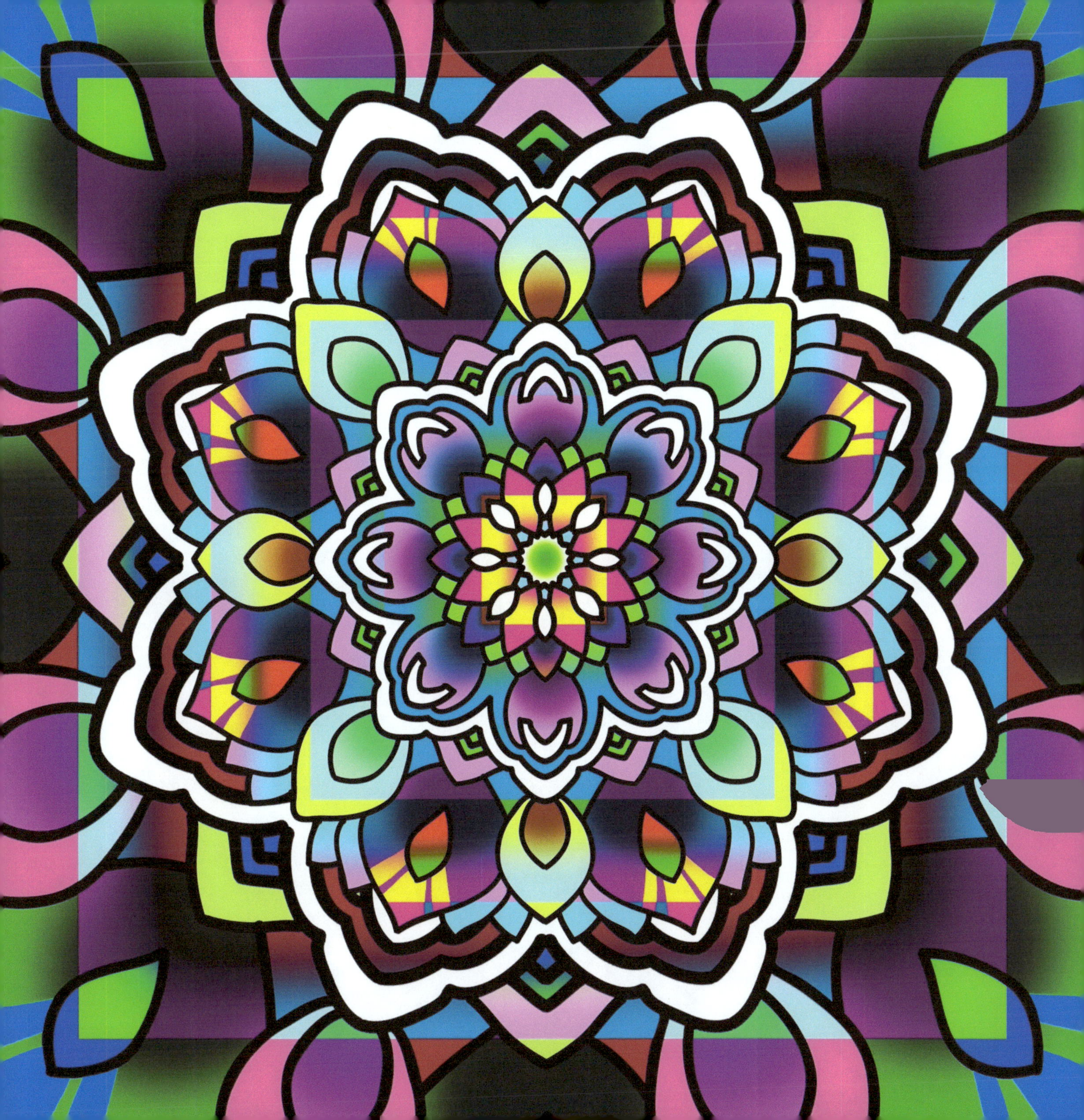

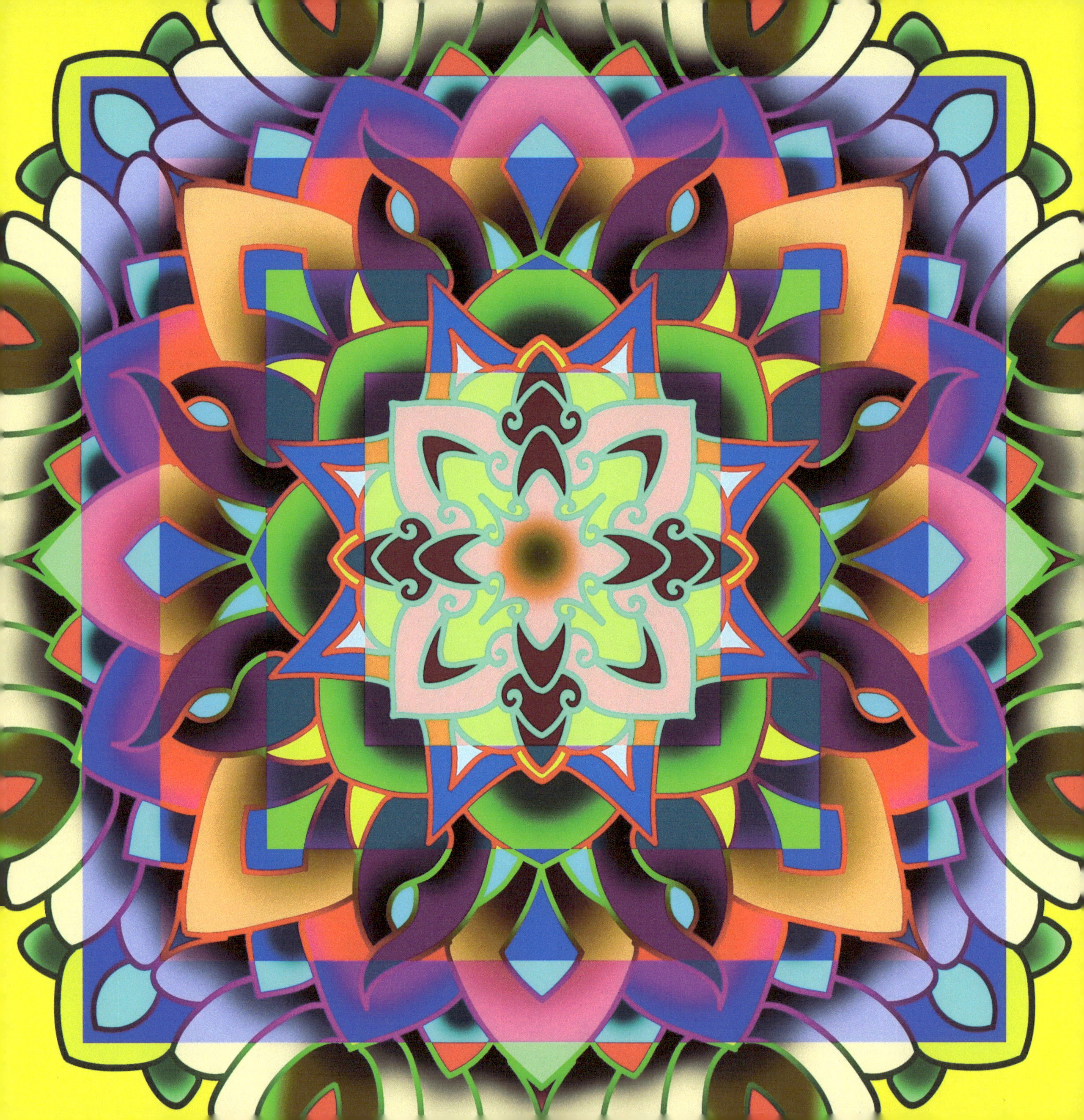

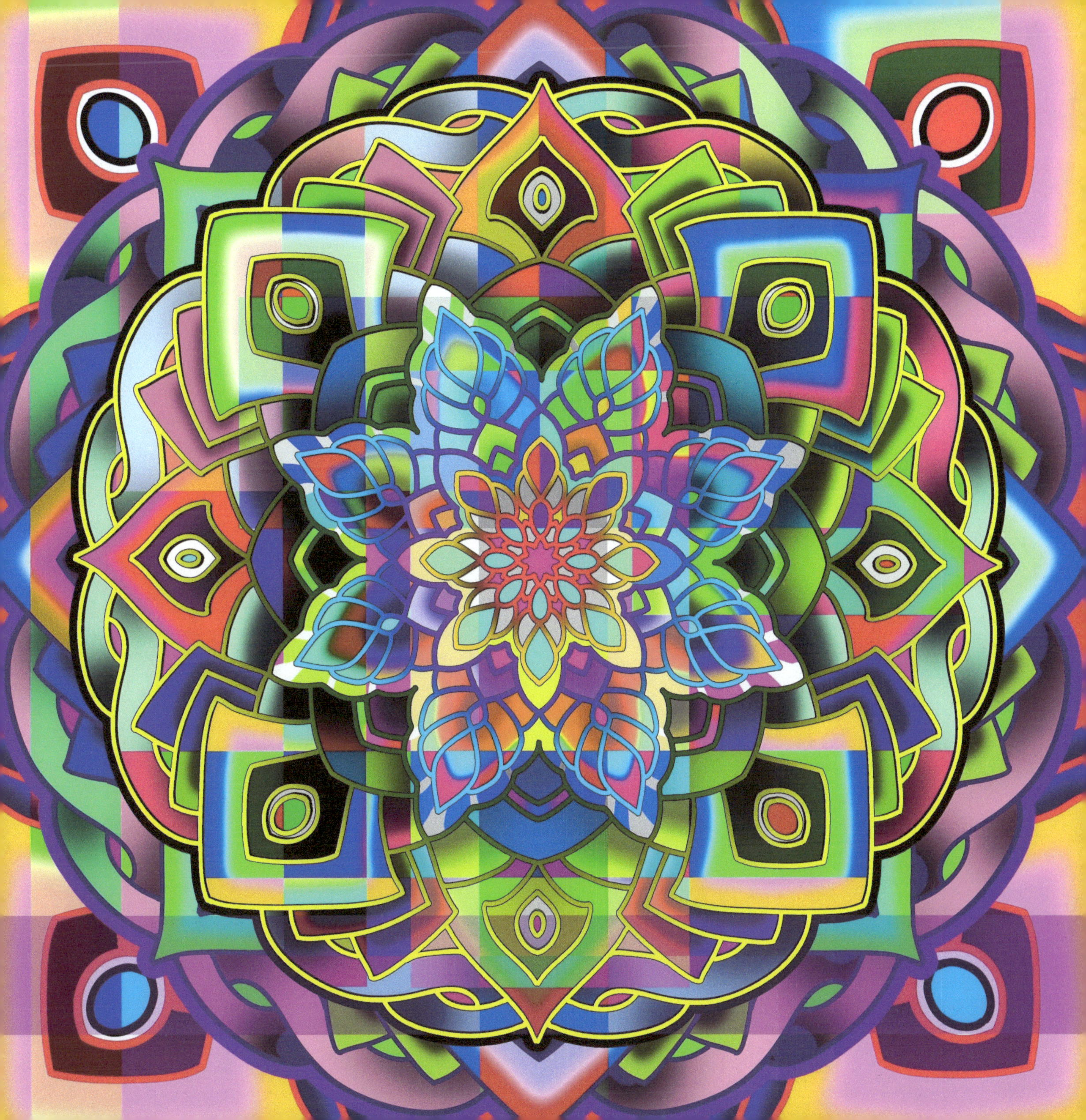

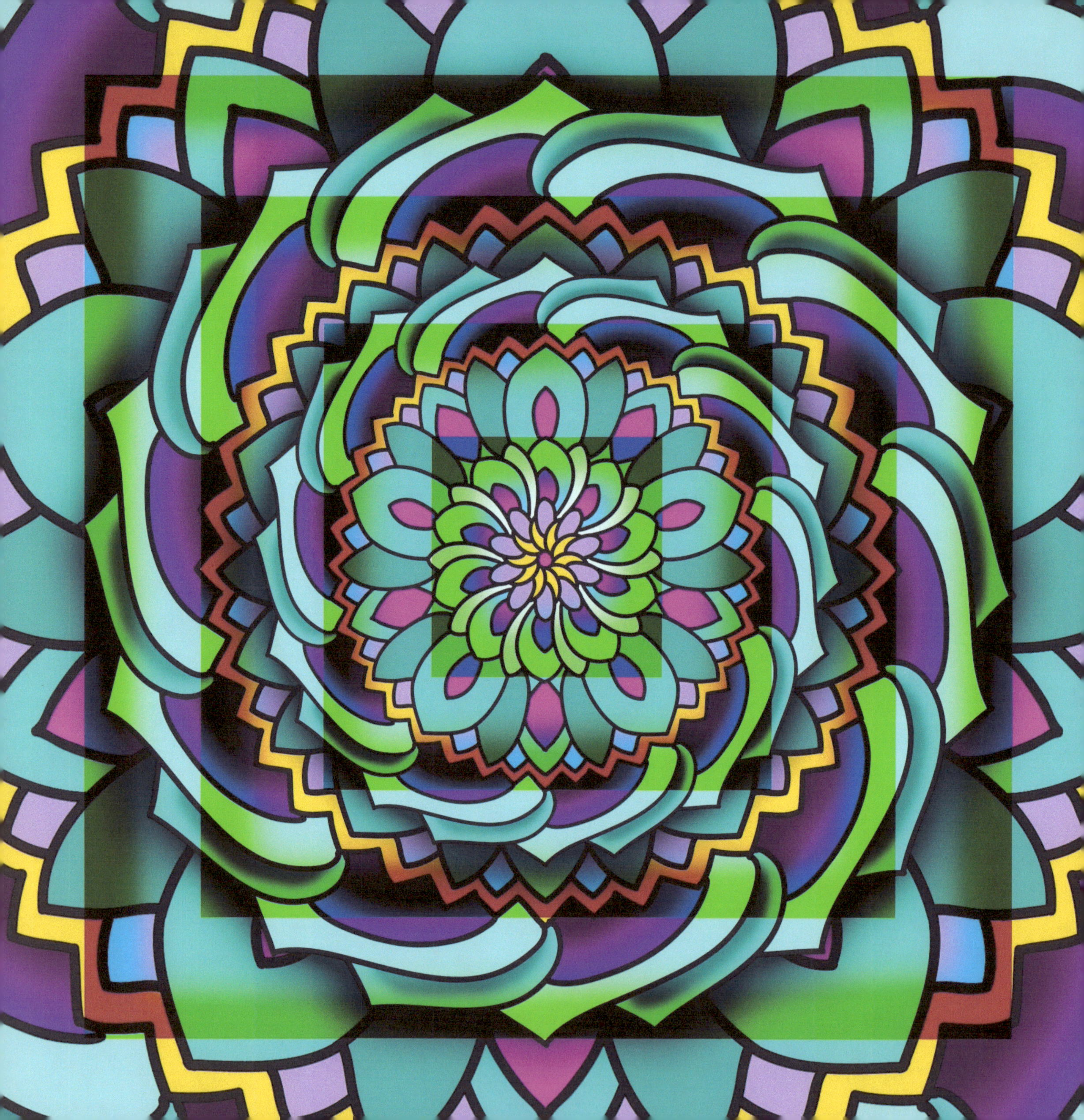

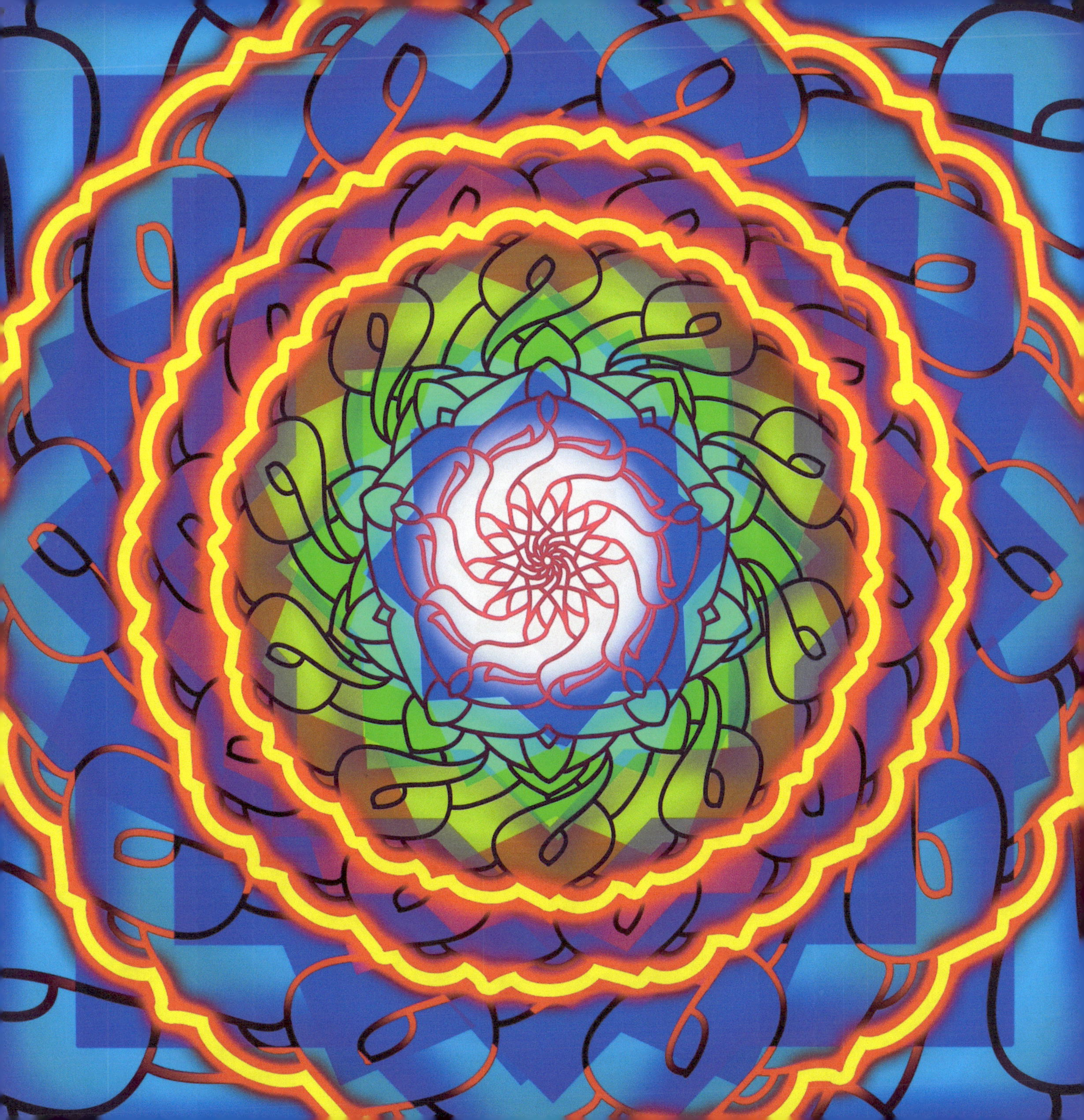

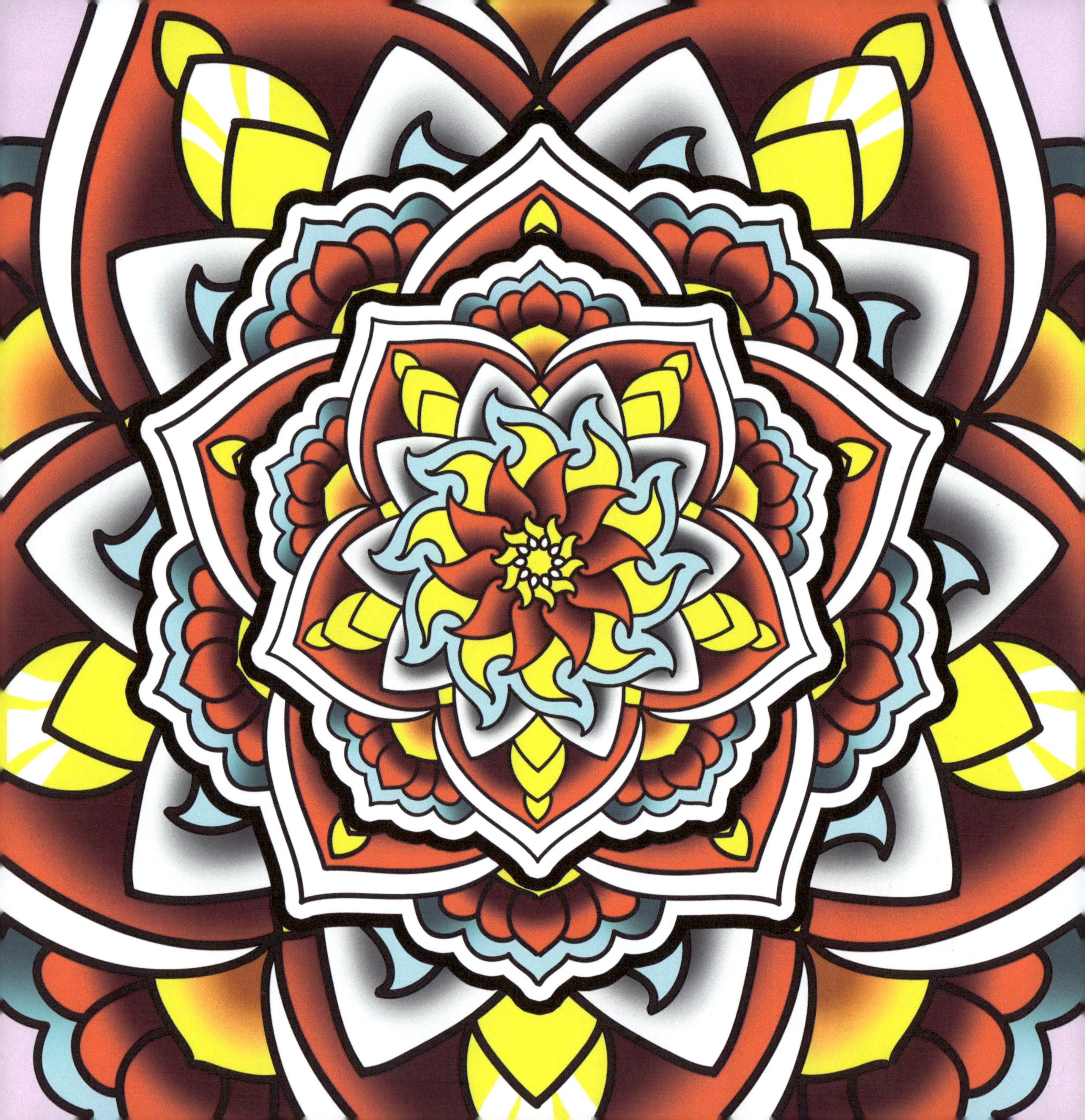

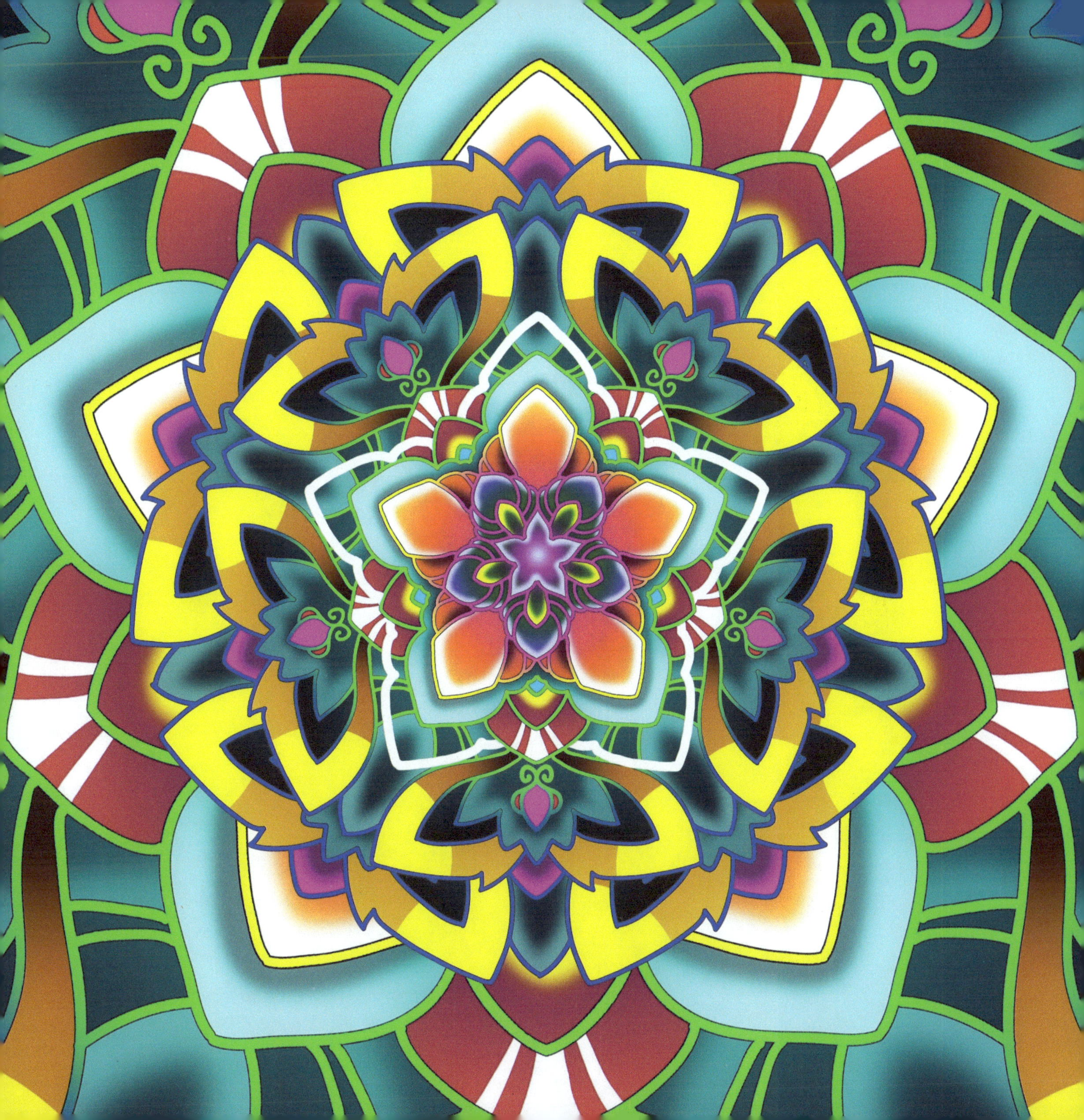

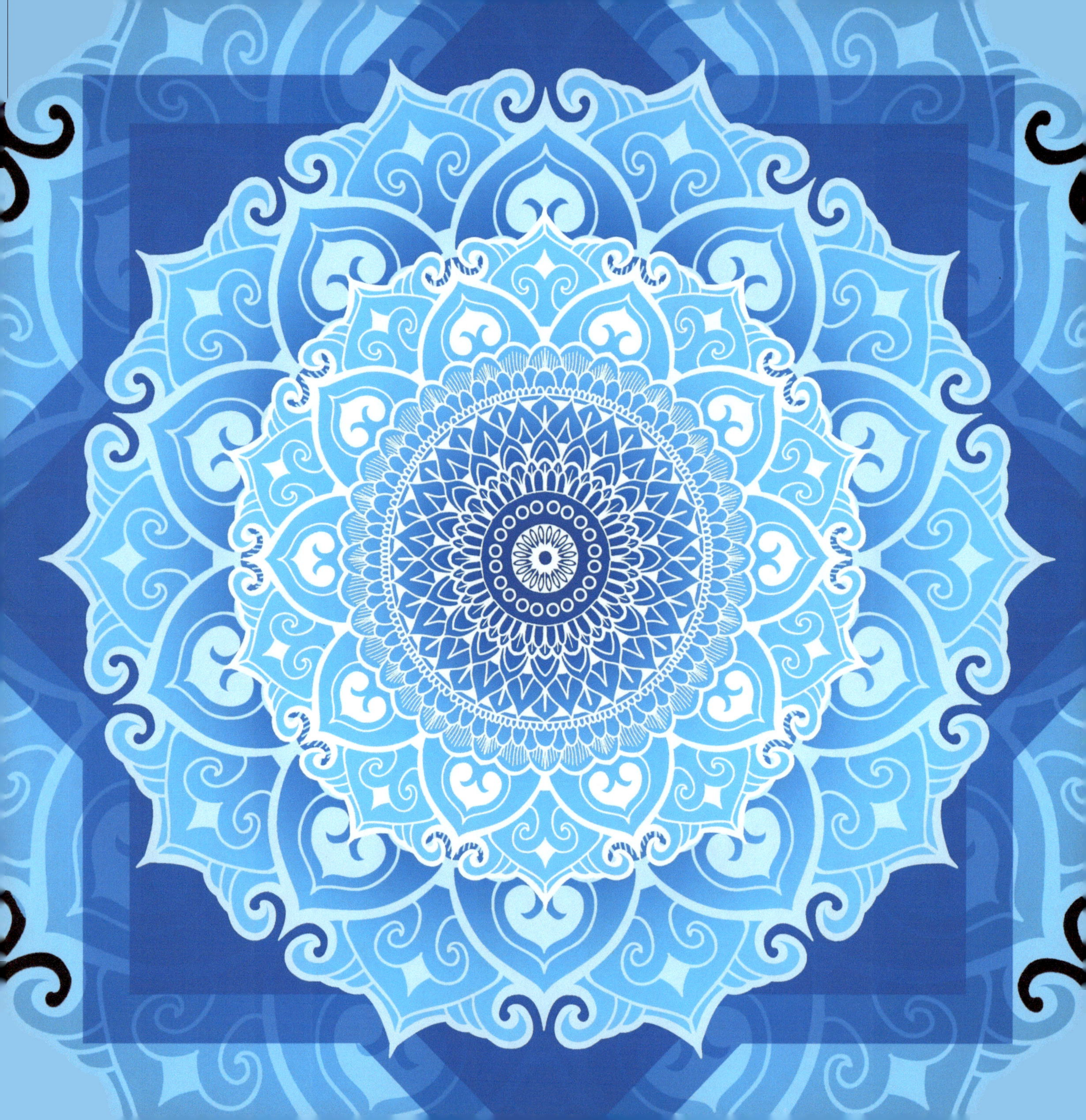

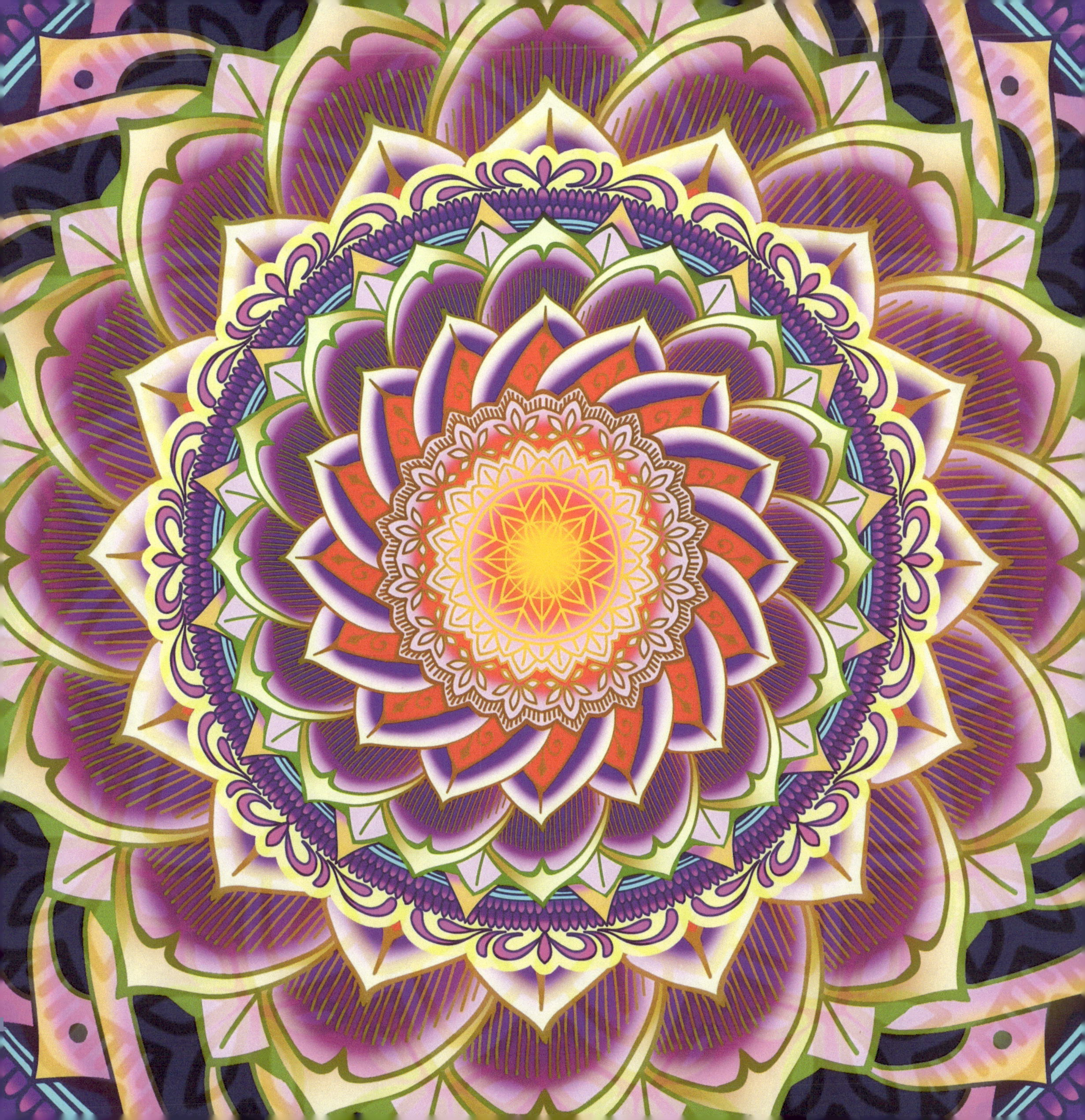

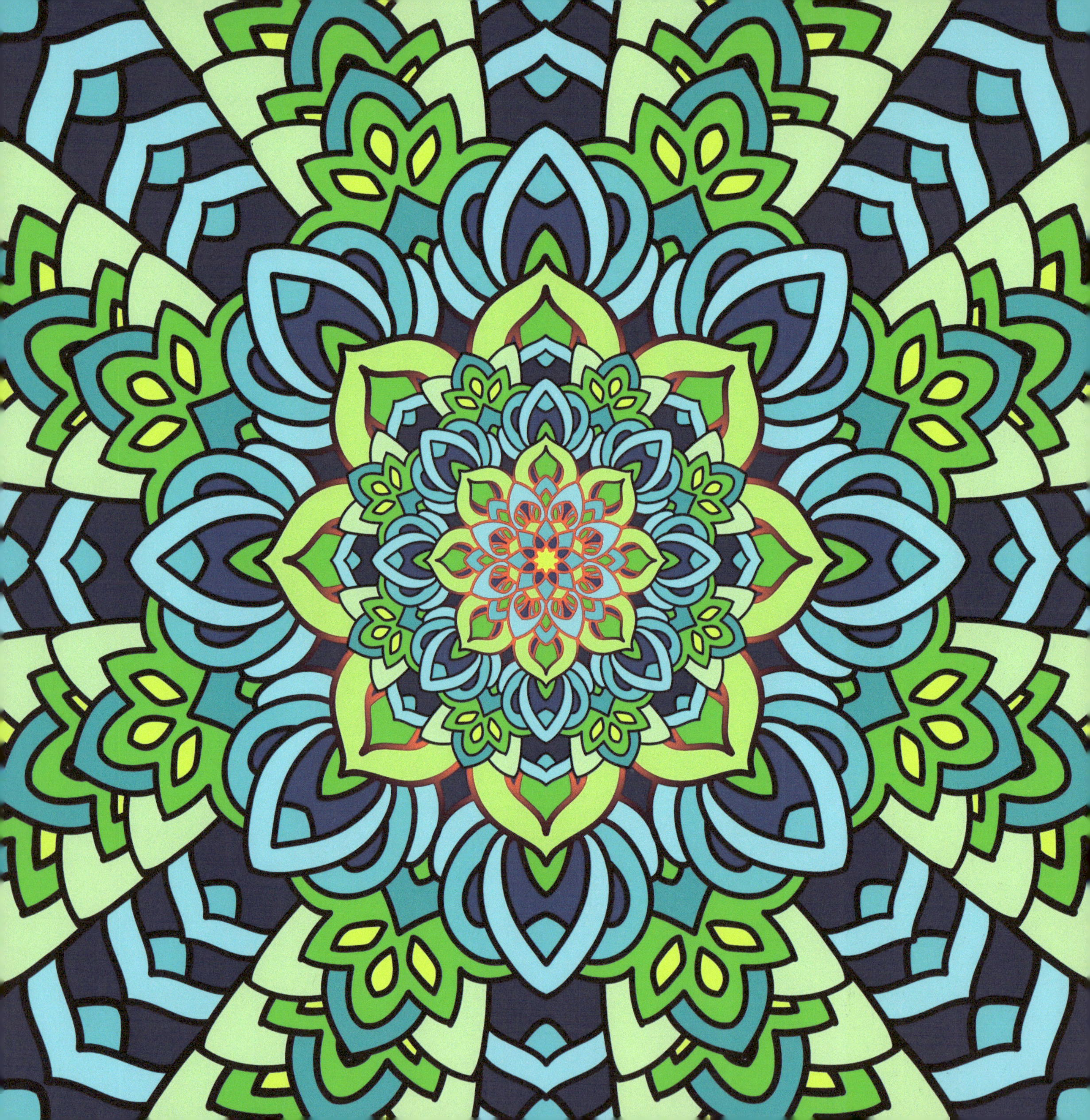

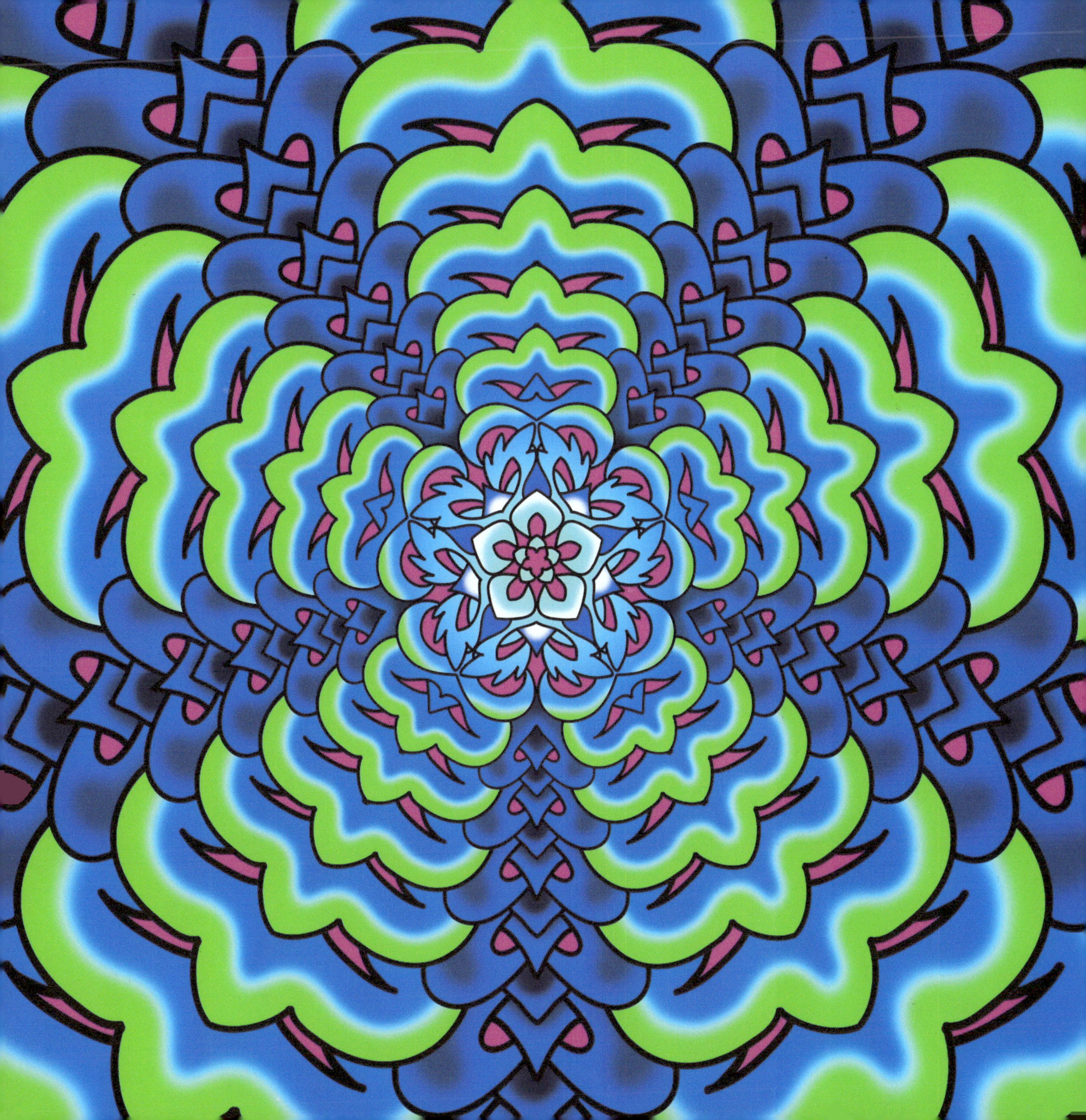

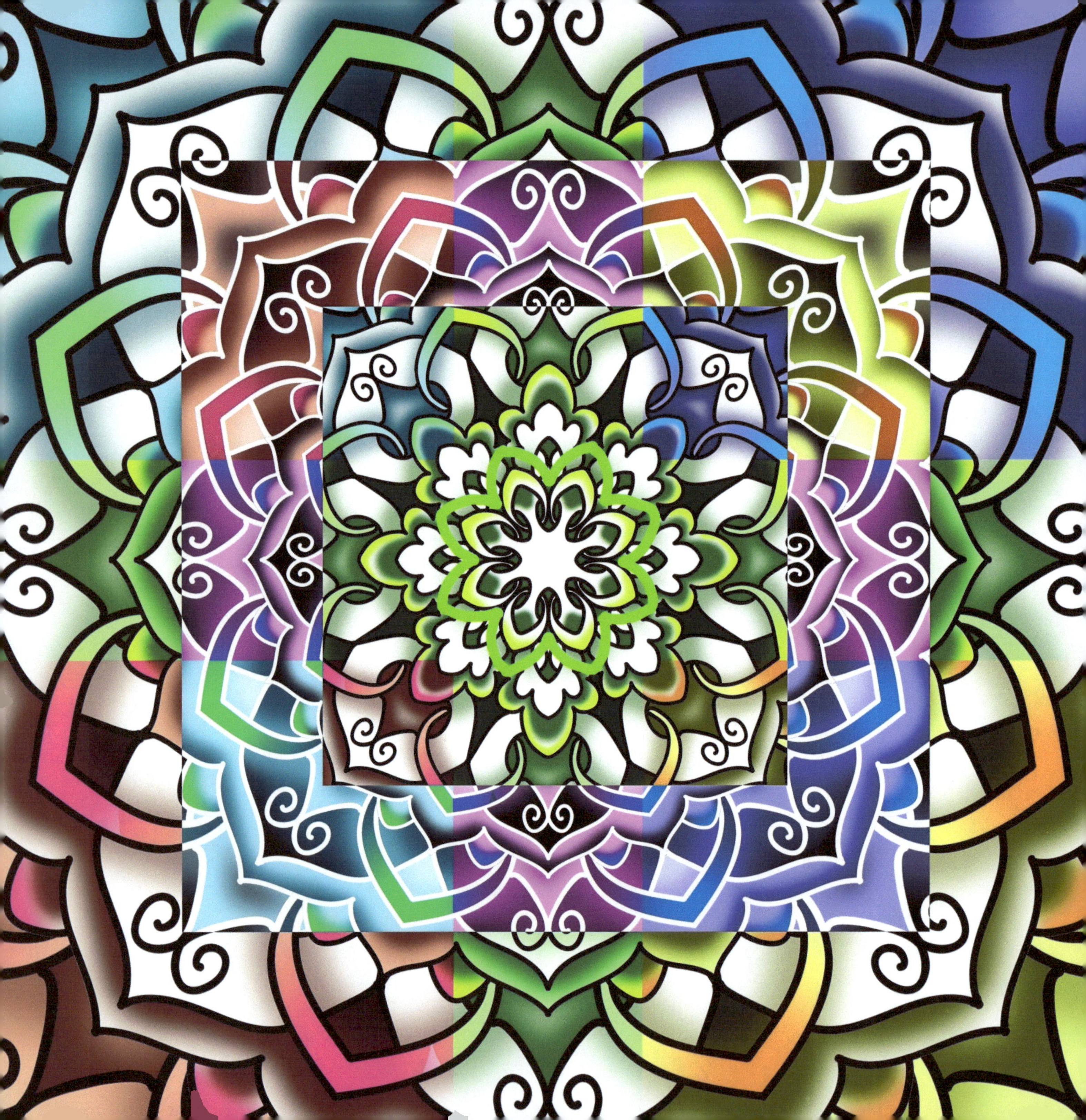

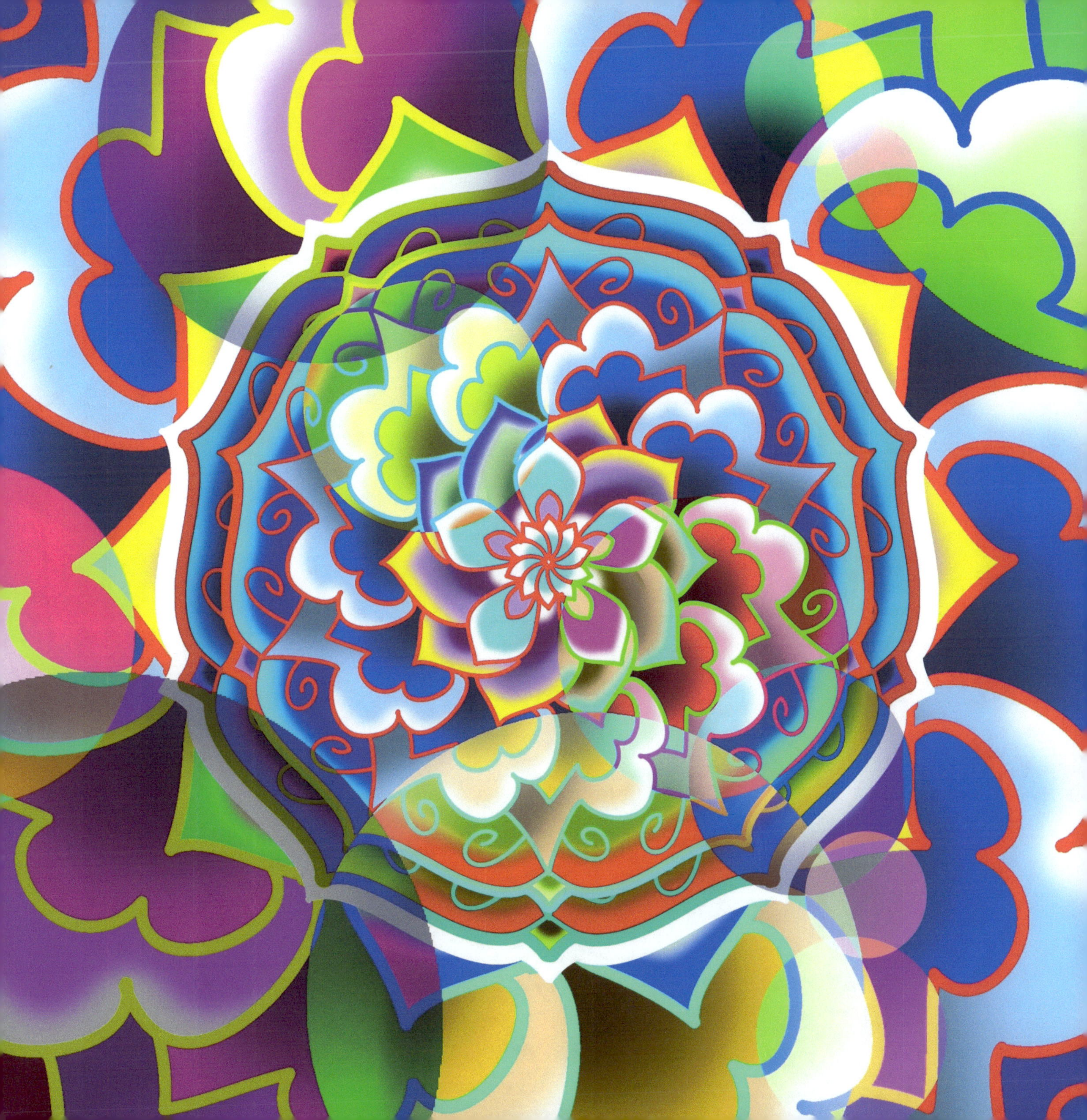

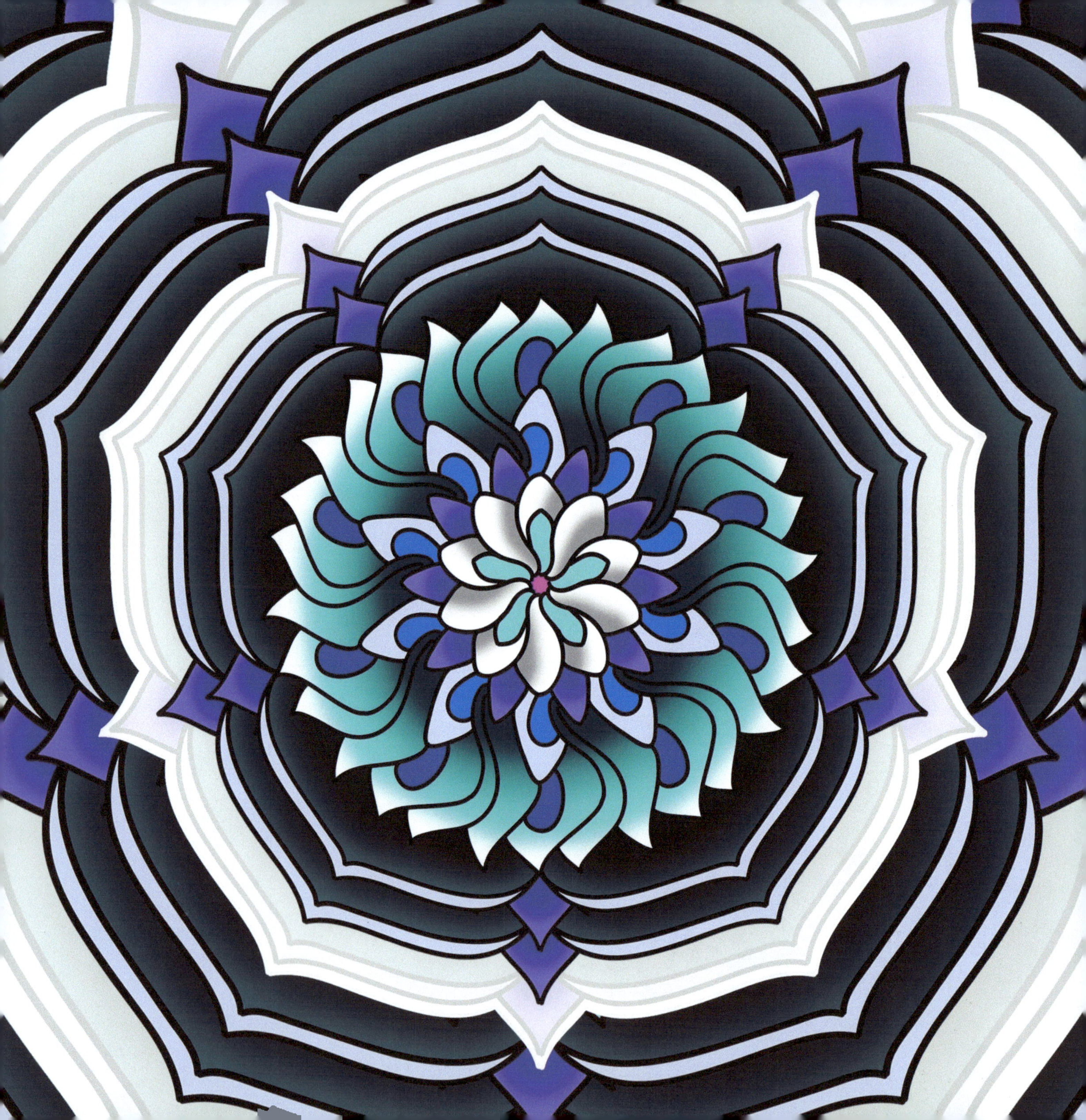

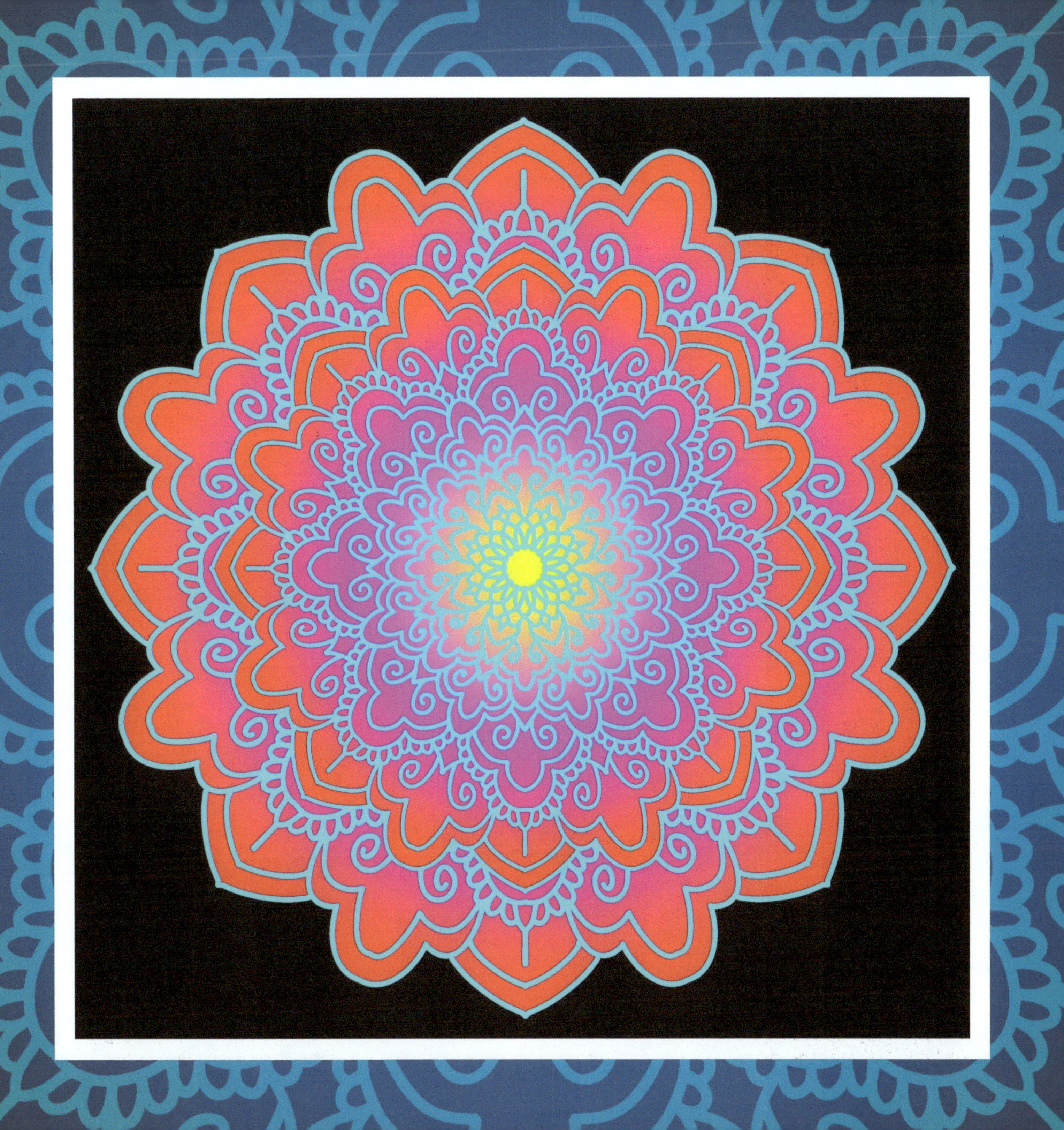

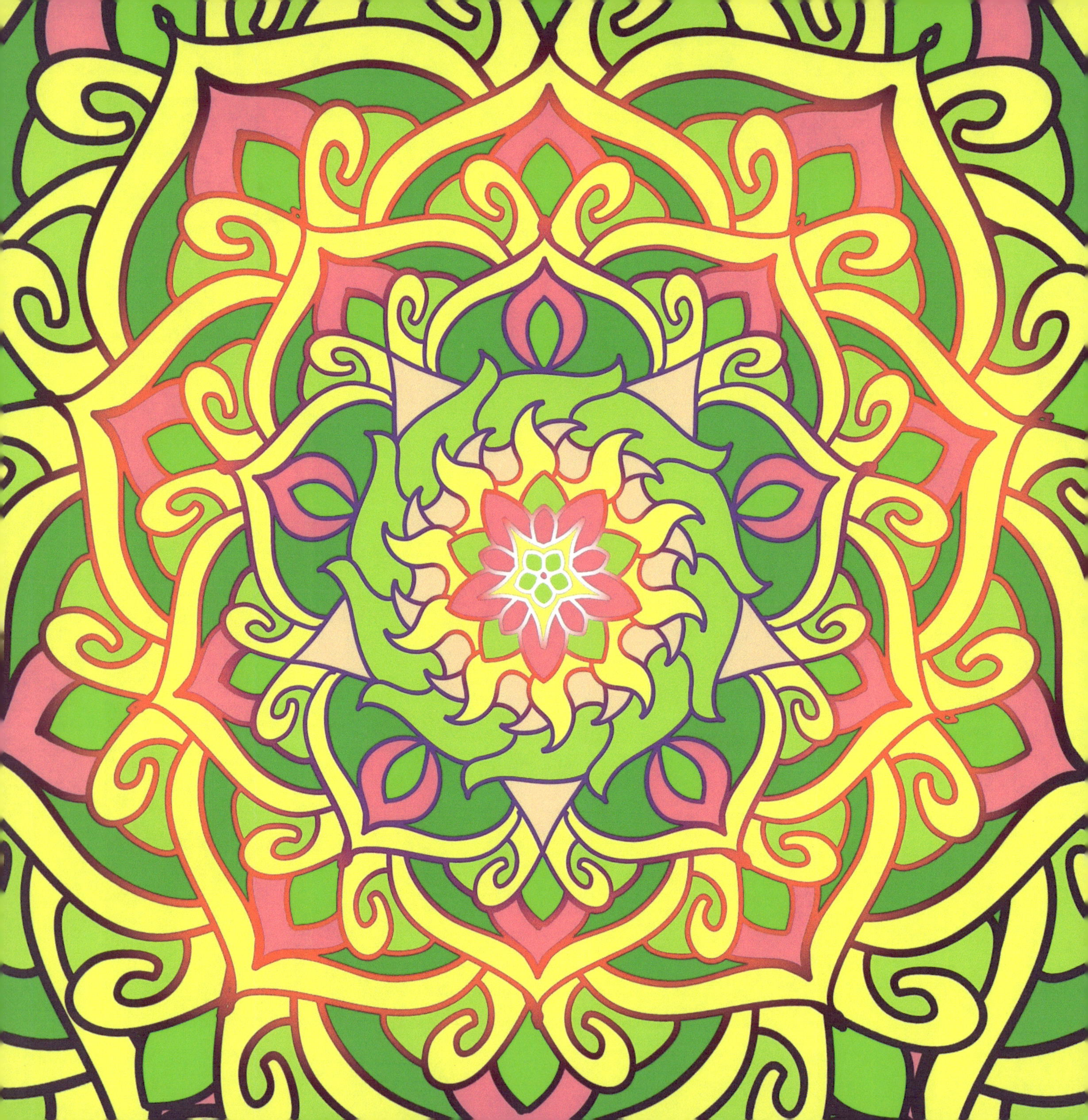

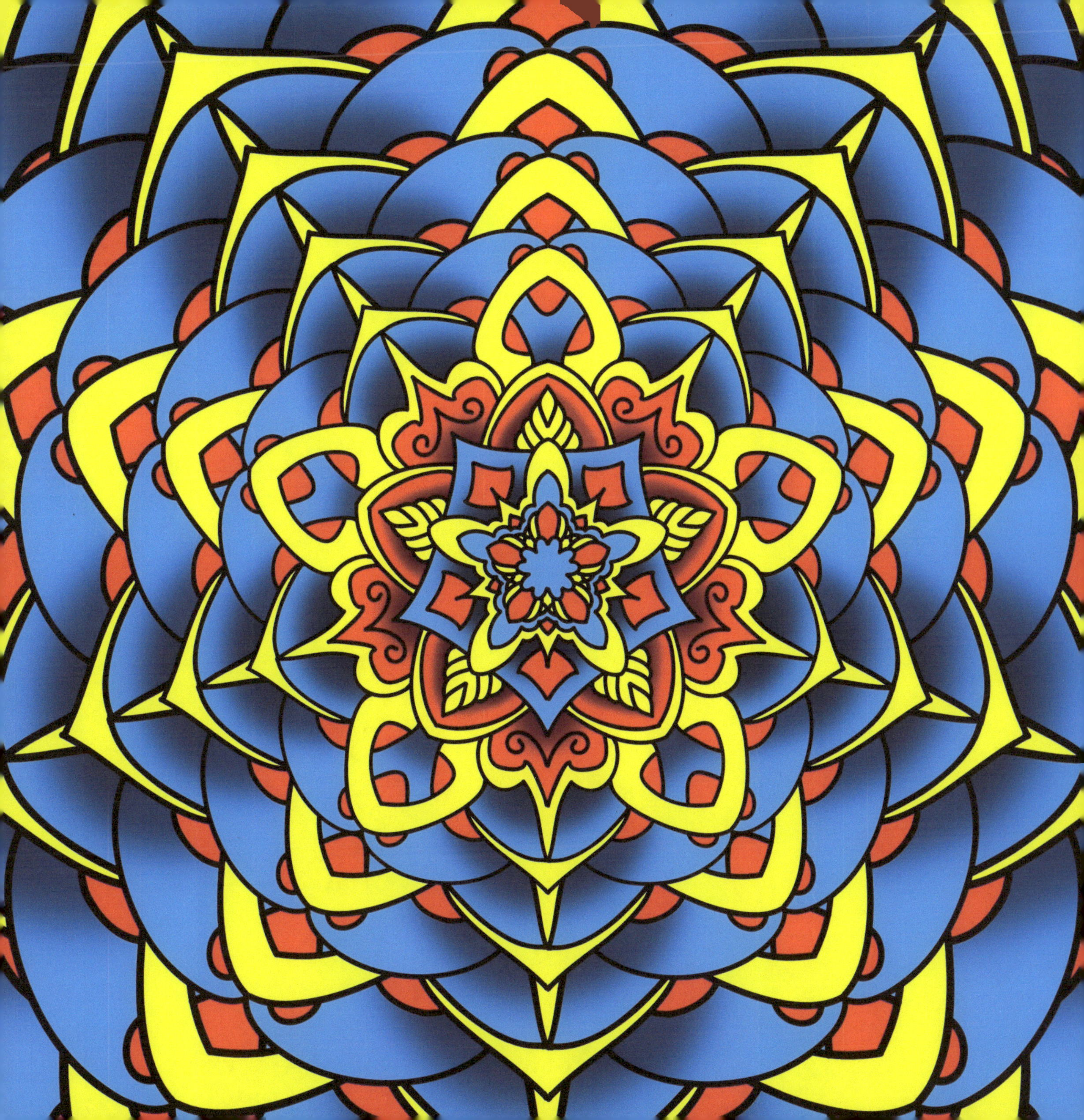

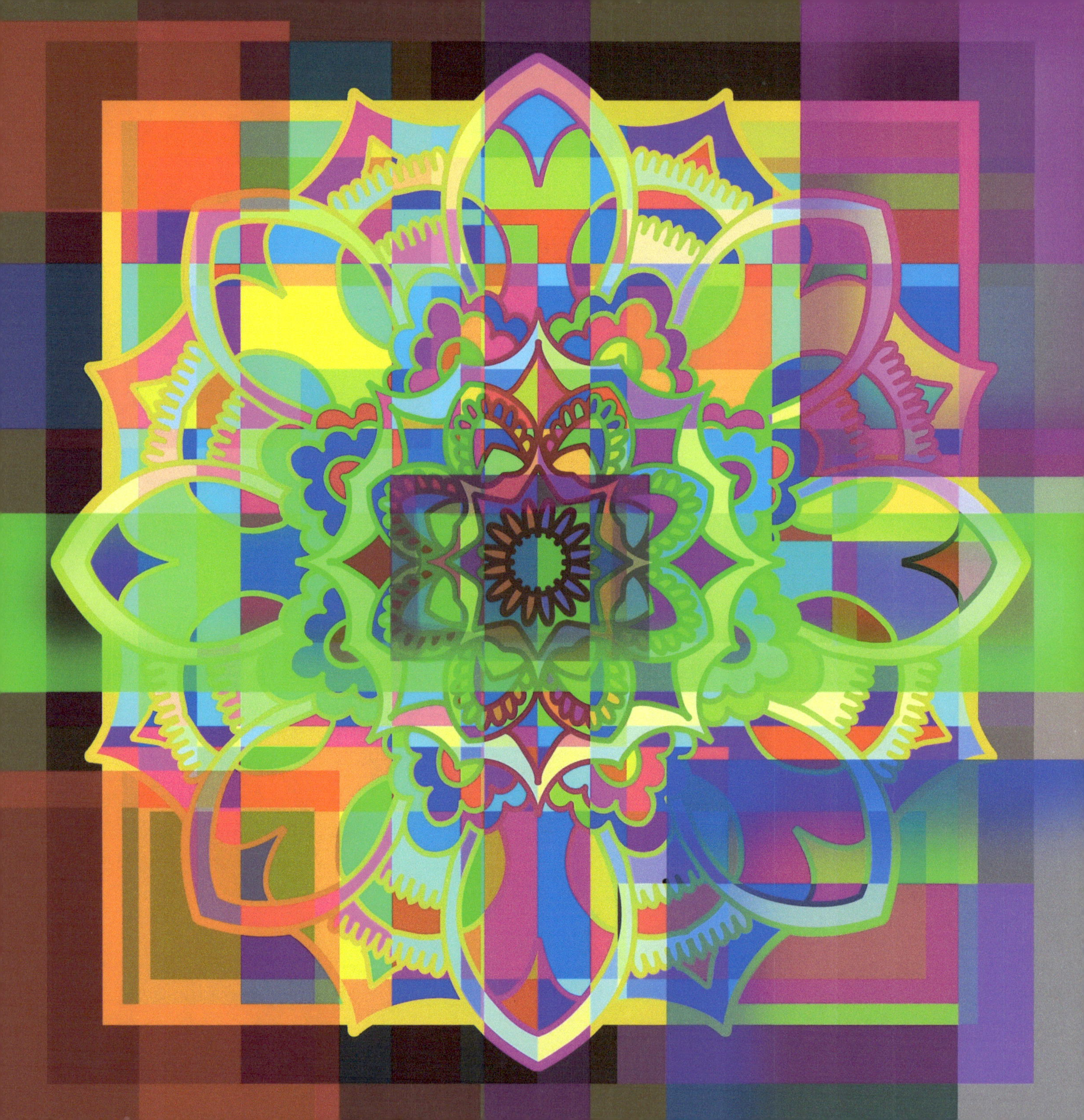

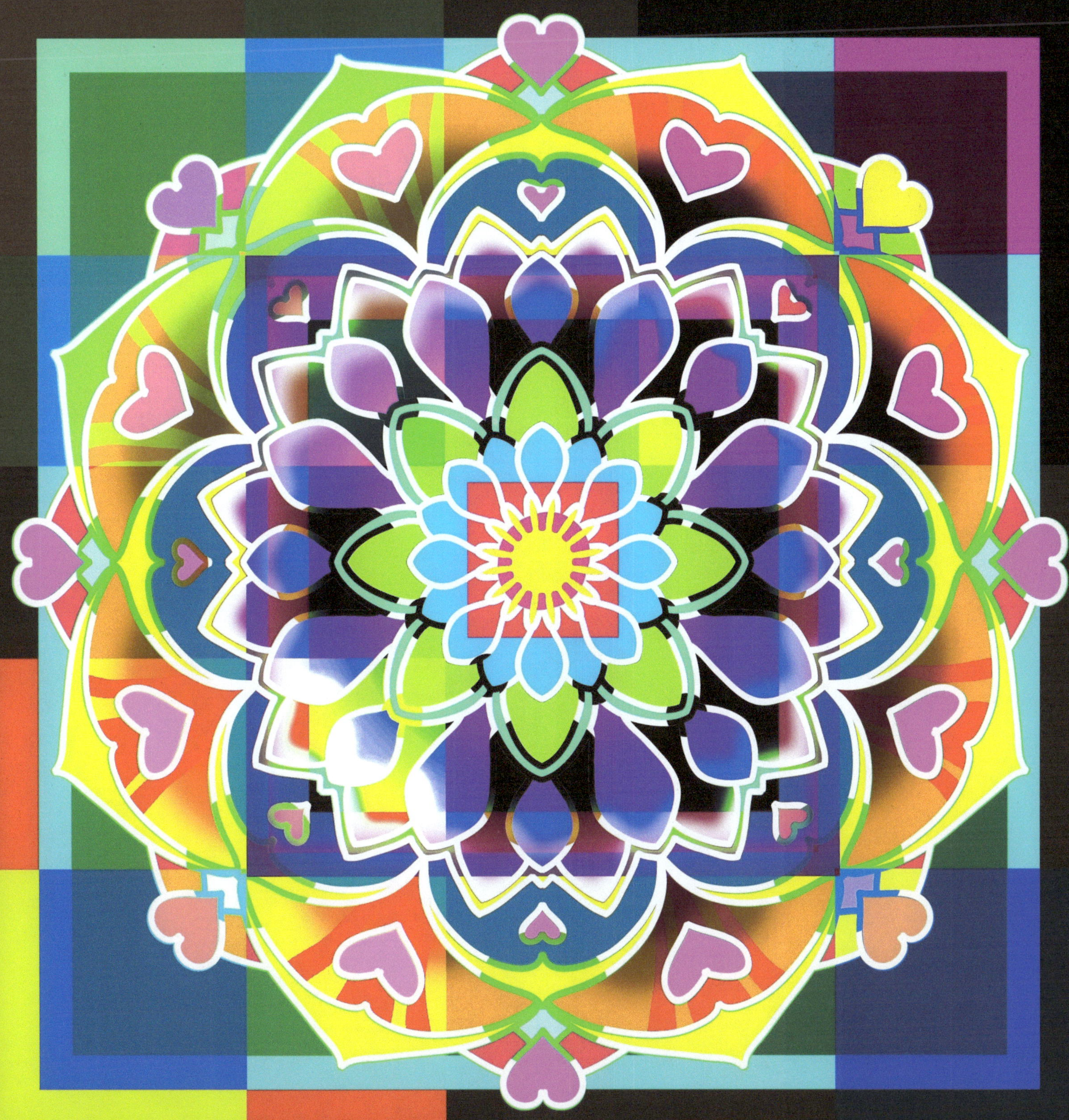

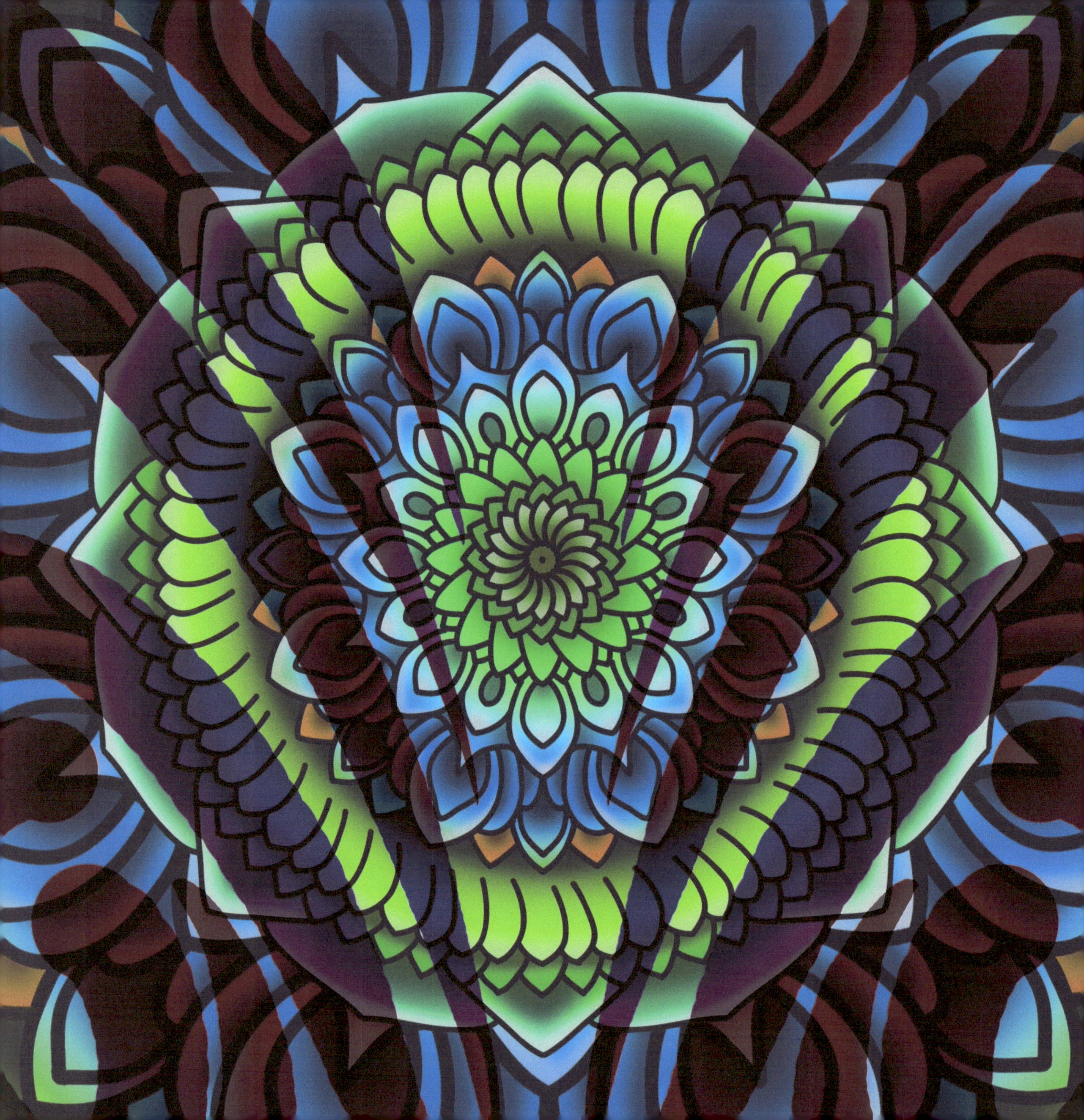

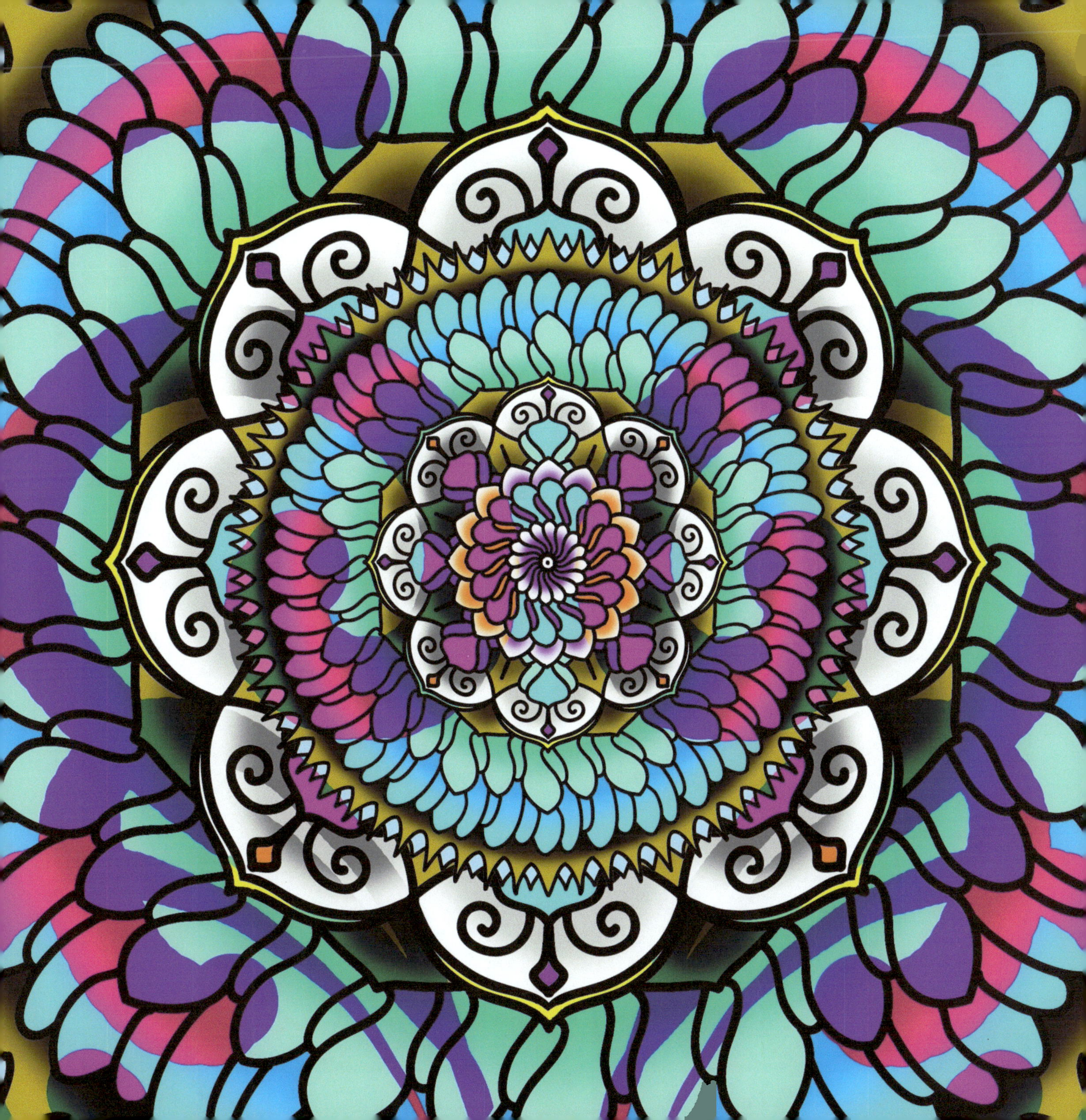

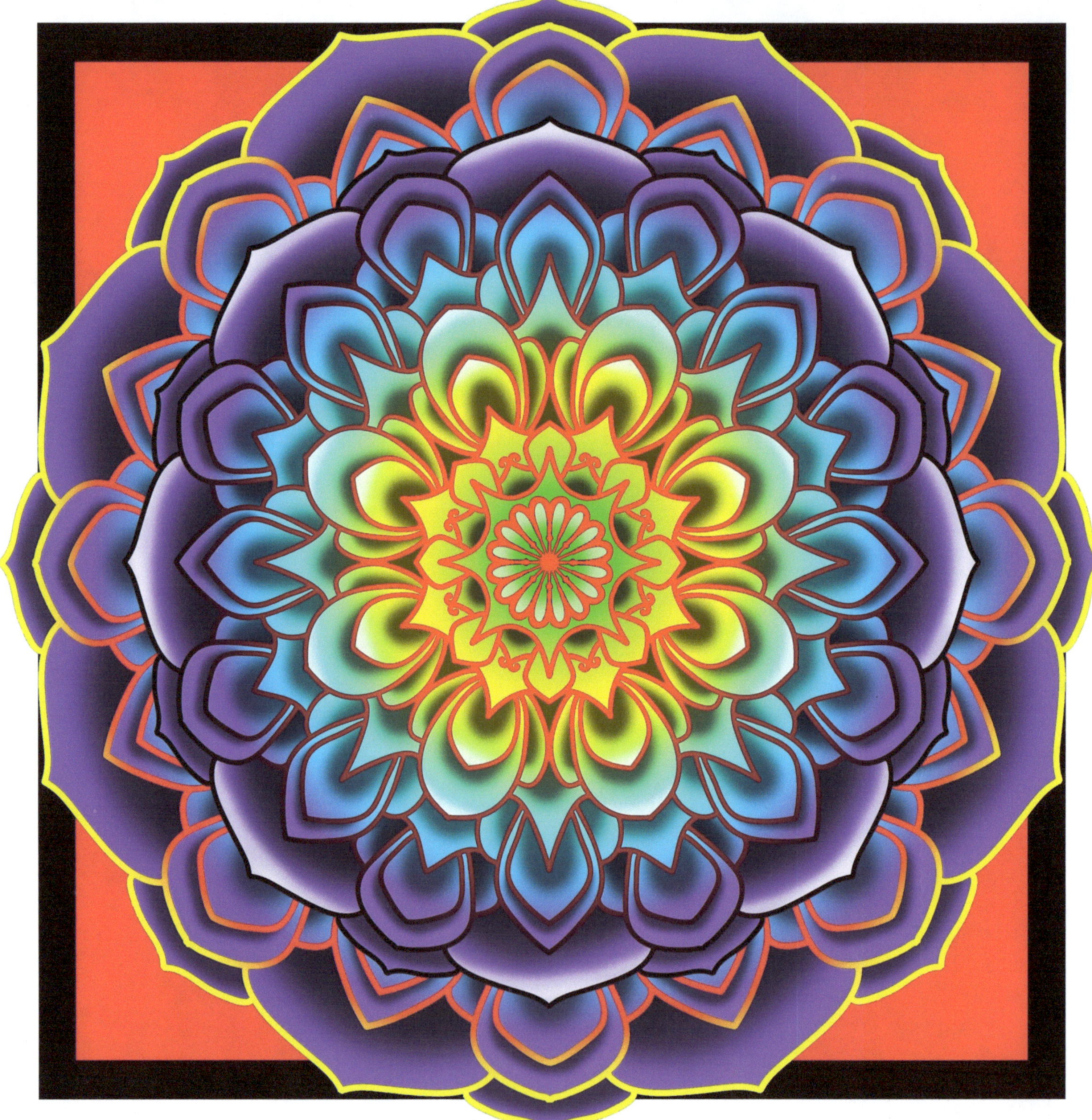

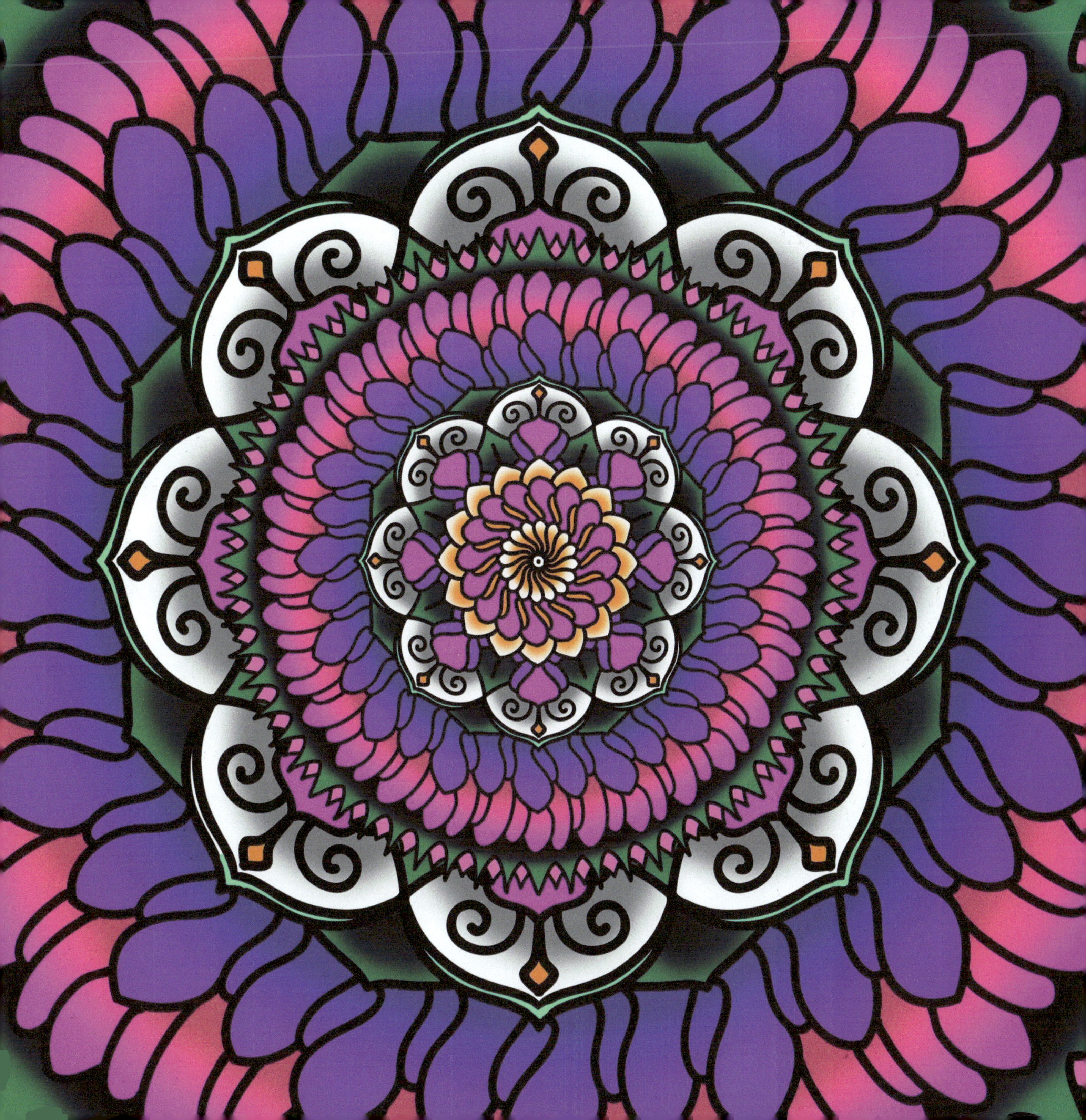

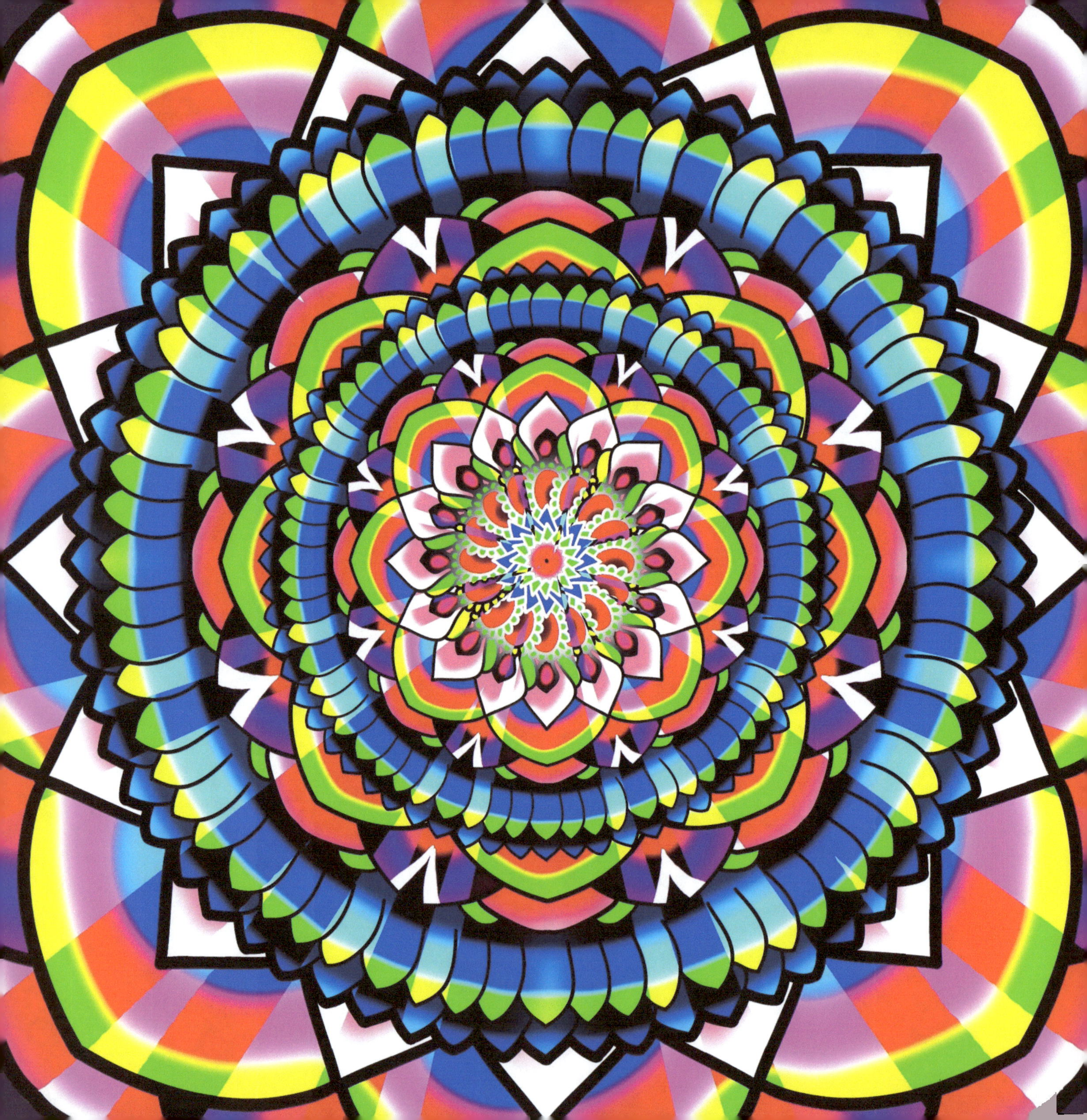

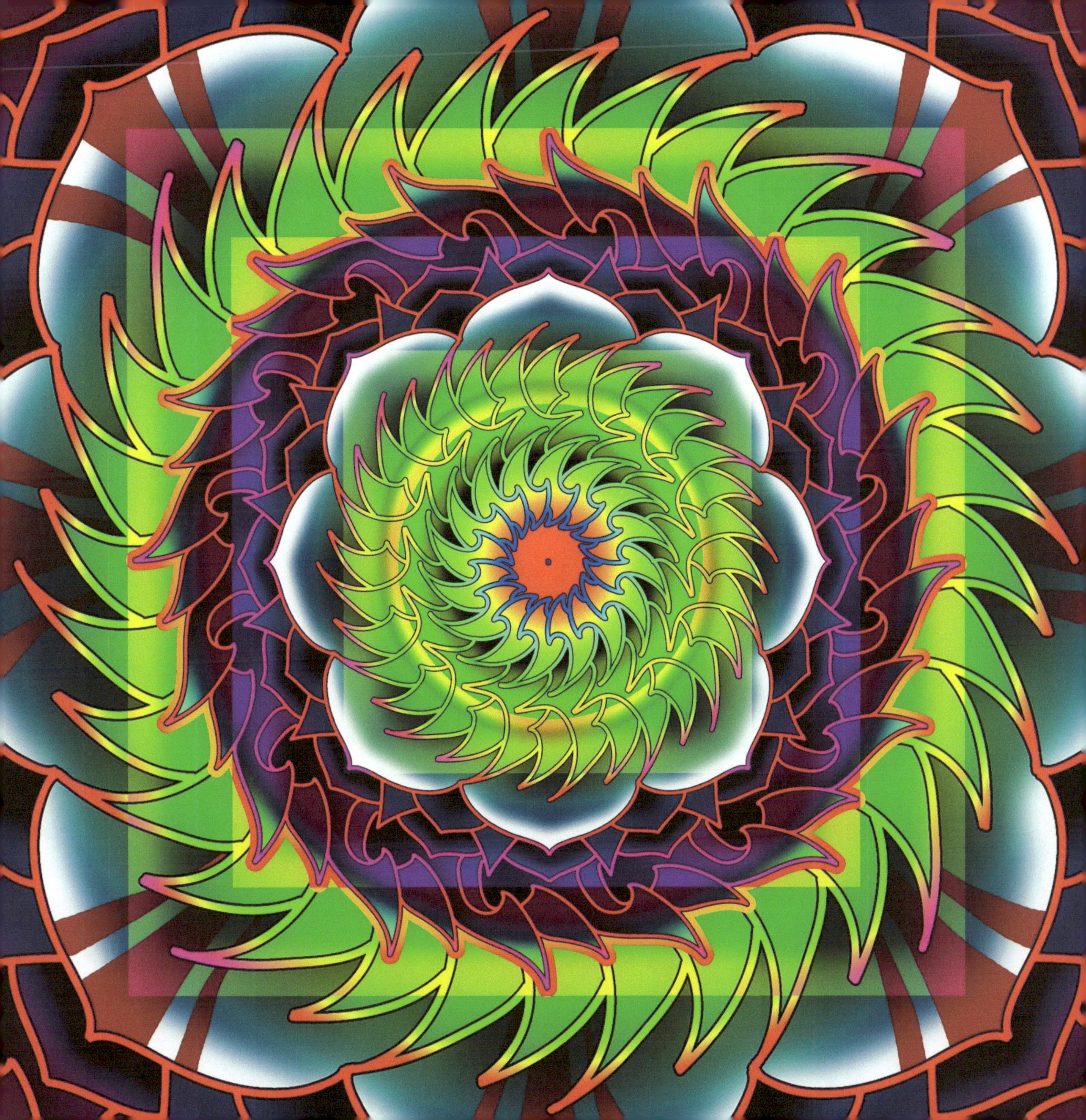

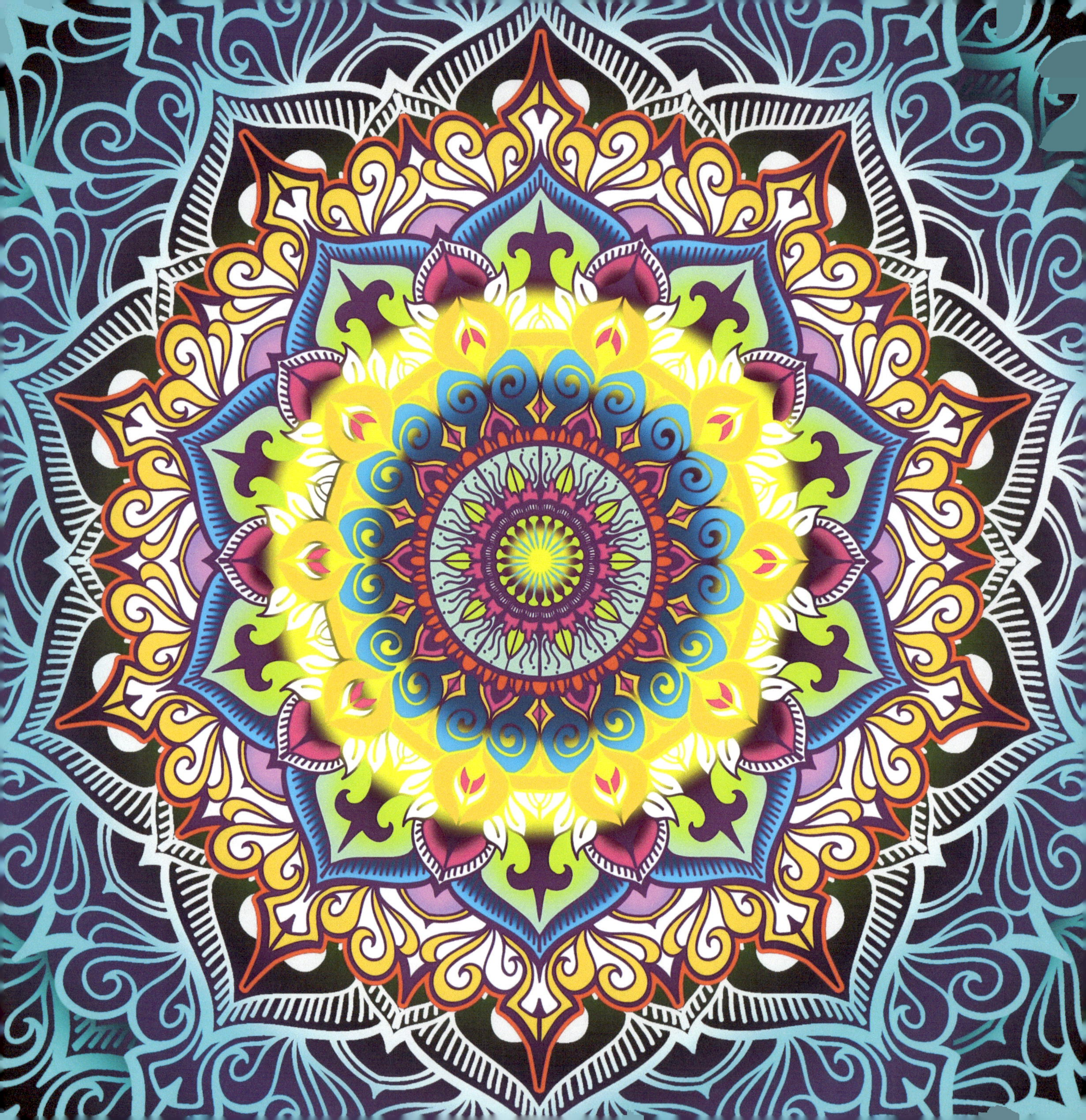

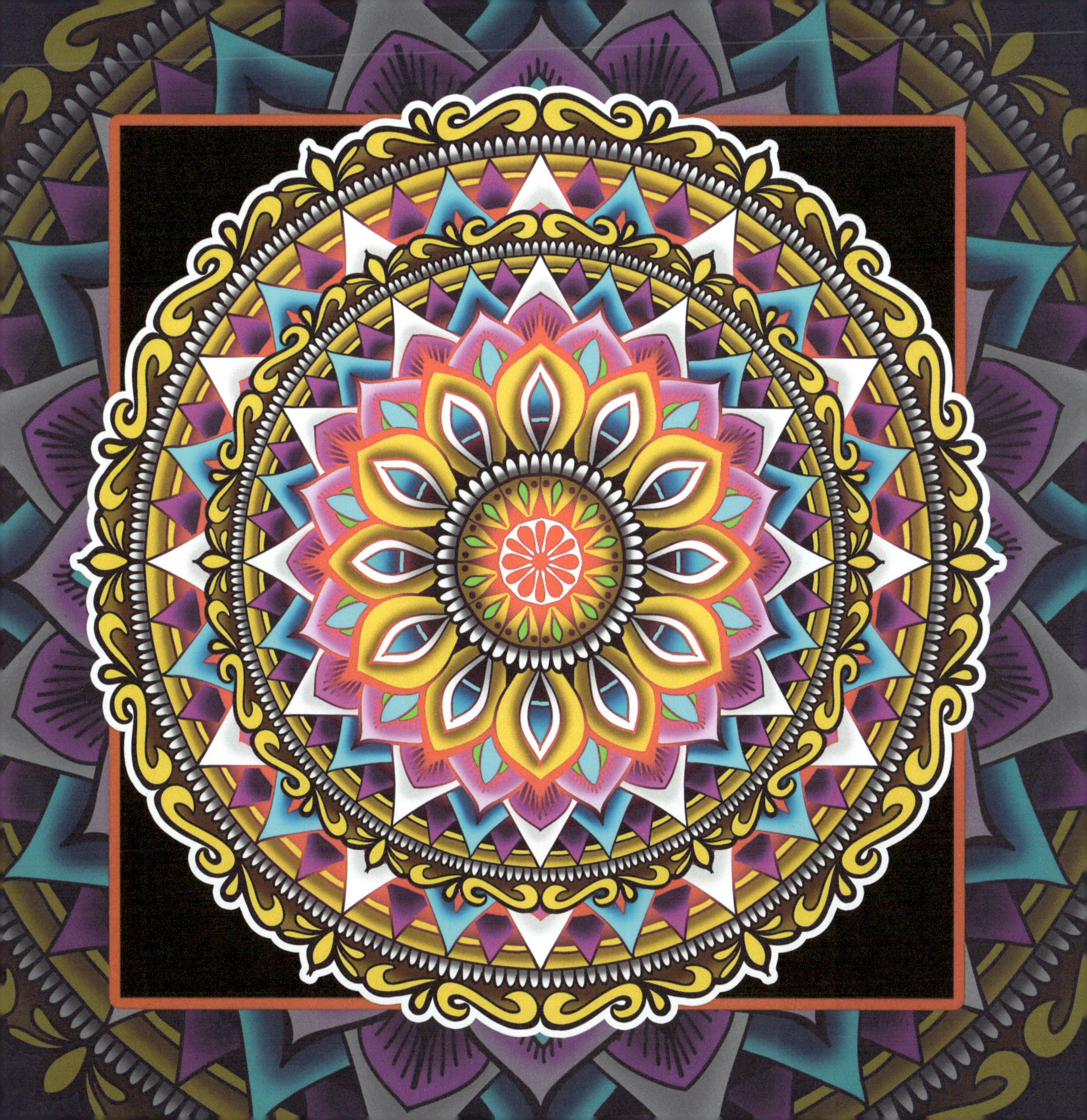

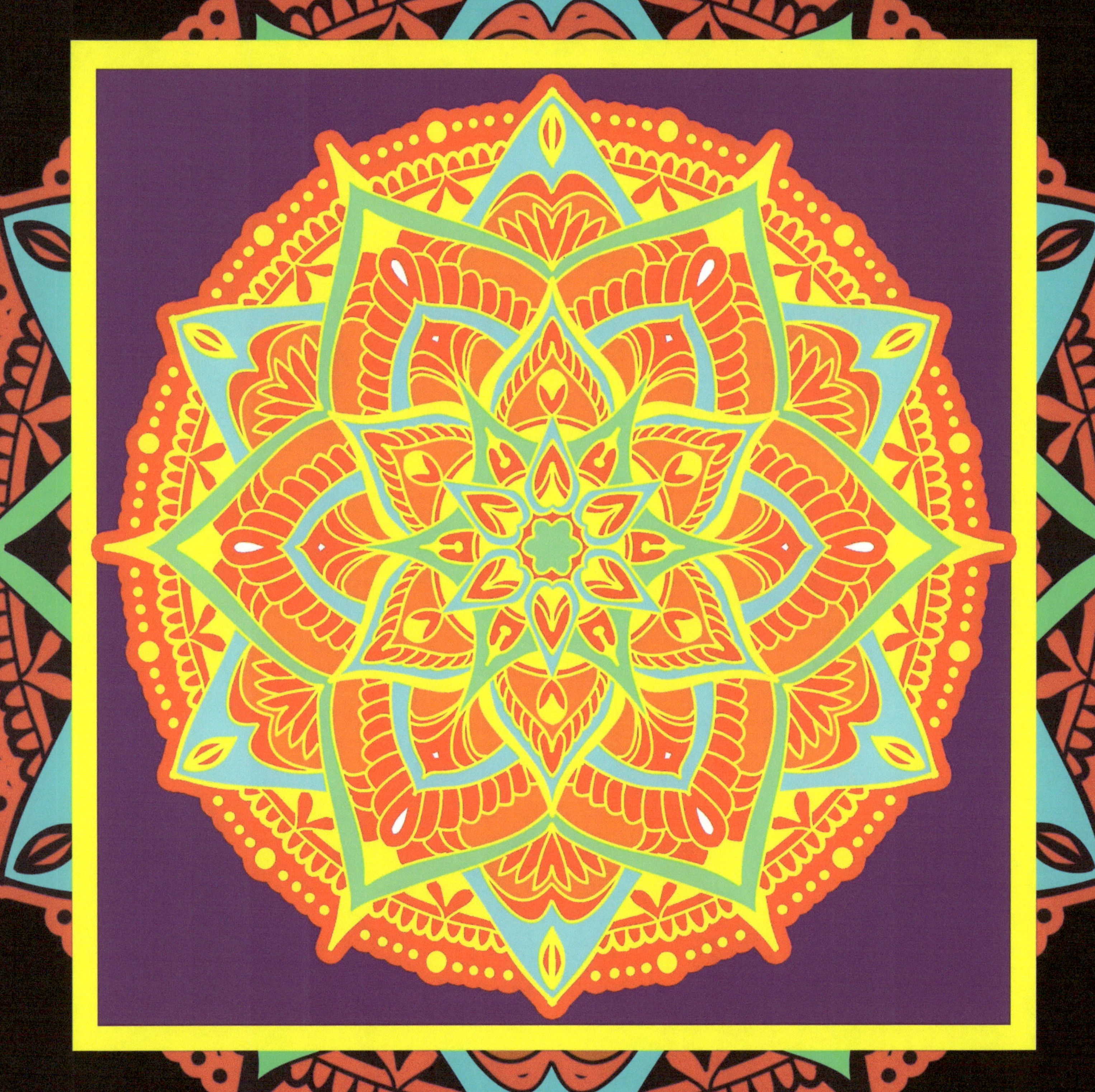

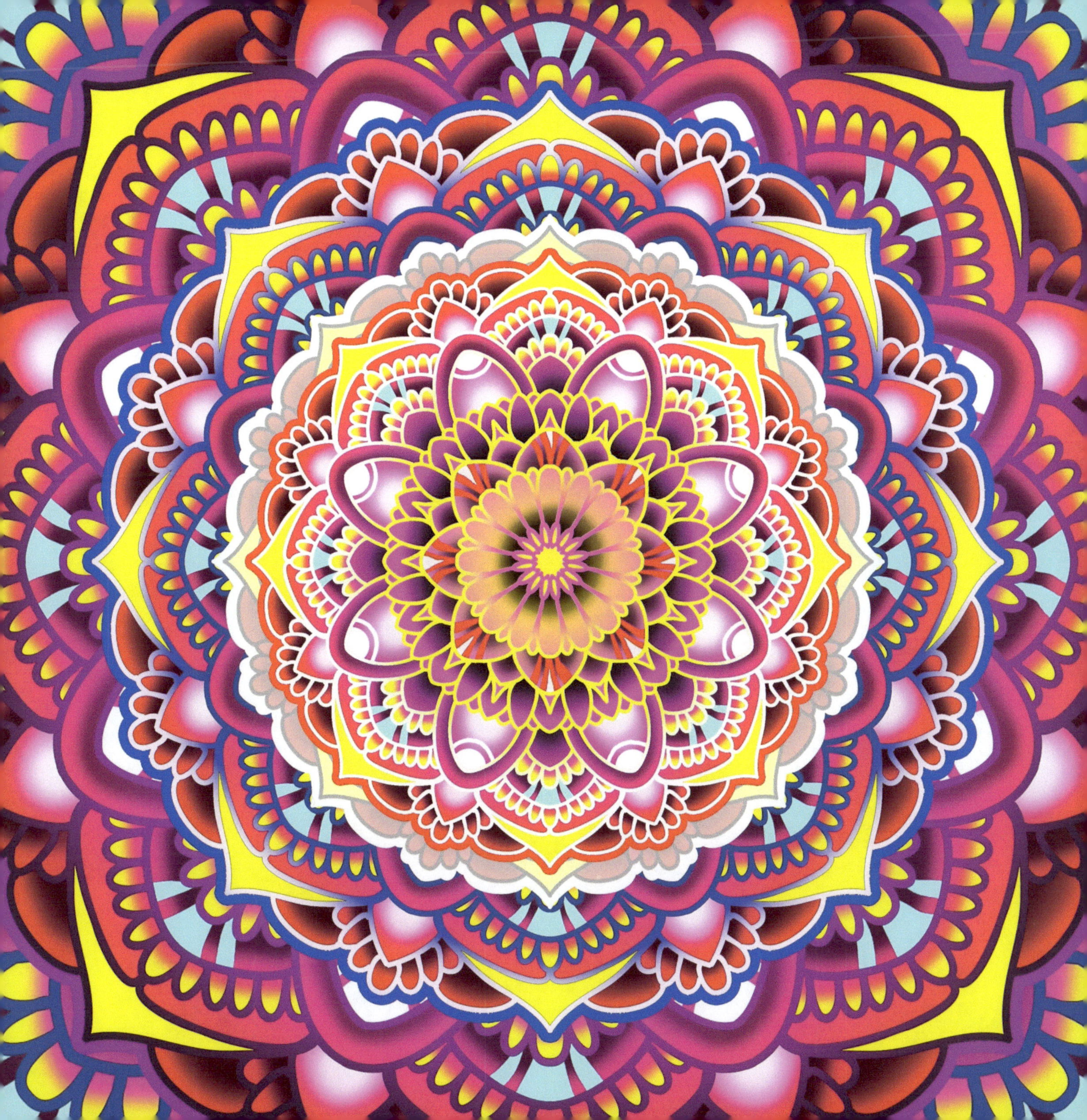

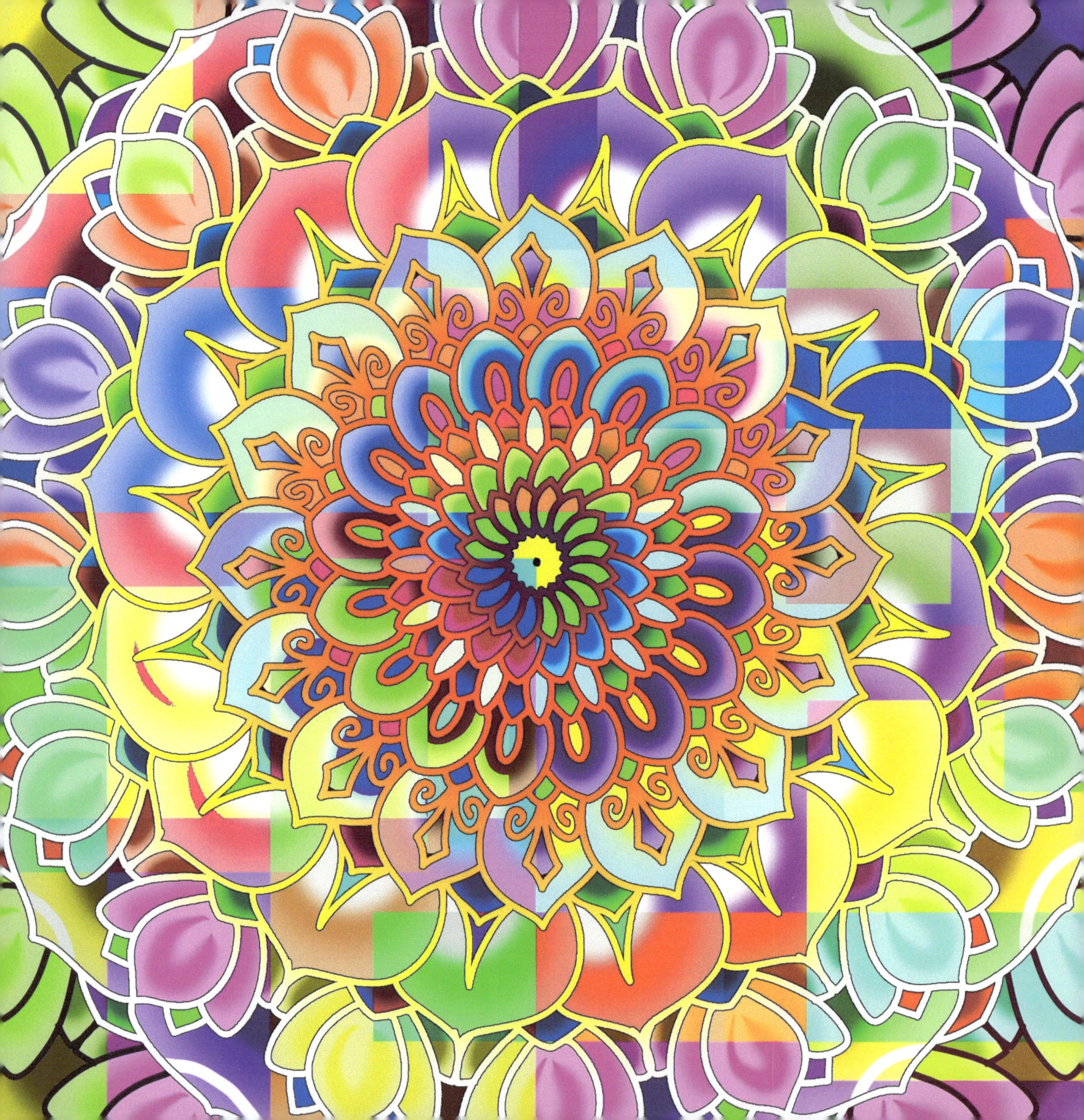

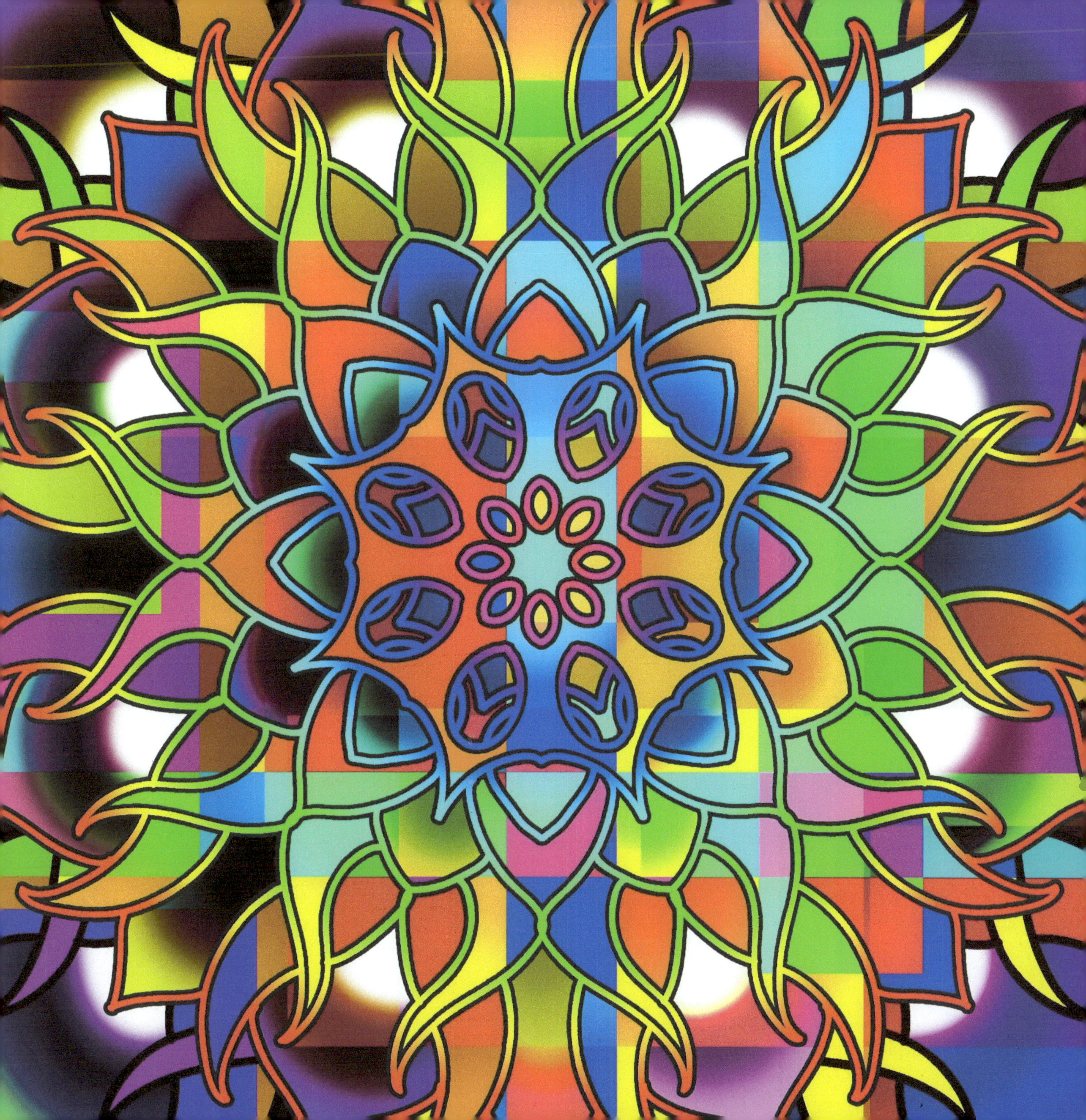

www.ingramcontent.com/pod-product-compliance
Lightning Source LLC
LaVergne TN
LVHW070216110826
845147LV00003B/583

* 9 7 8 1 9 4 8 1 8 7 2 8 2 *